THE LAND BEYOND THE FOREST

A.T.L.

AMERICAN THEATER IN LITERATURE

Advisory Board

Gordon Davidson
Kenward Elmslie
David Henry Hwang
Jerome Lawrence
Richard Nelson
Eric Overmyer
Suzan-Lori Parks
Carey Perloff
Peter Sellars
Fiona Templeton
Mac Wellman

Douglas Messerli, *Publisher*

The Land Beyond the Forest
DRACULA *and* SWOOP

Mac Wellman

SUN & MOON PRESS
A SOHO REP BOOK
LOS ANGELES • 1995

Sun & Moon Press
A Program of The Contemporary Arts Educational Project, Inc.
a nonprofit corporation
6026 Wilshire Boulevard, Los Angeles, California 90036

This edition first published in paperback in 1995 by Sun & Moon Press
10 9 8 7 6 5 4 3 2 1
FIRST EDITION
©1995 by Mac Wellman
Biographical material ©1995 by Sun & Moon Press
All rights reserved

For all professional and production rights to *Dracula* and *Swoop,*
and for associated rights, permission inquiries, and other media rights,
please contact the author's agent, Brad Kalos, International Creative
Management, 40 West 57th Street, 18th Floor, New York, NY 10019

This book was made possible, in part, through an operational grant from the
Andrew W. Mellon Foundation and through contributions to
The Contemporary Arts Educational Project, Inc.,
a nonprofit corporation.

Cover: *Arch of Triumph,* René Magritte (1960)
Design: Katie Messborn
Typography: Guy Bennett

LIBRARY OF CONGRESS CATALOGING IN PUBLICATION DATA
Wellman, Mac [John] [1945]
The Land Beyond the Forest: Dracula and Swoop / Mac Wellman.— 1st ed.
p. cm — (Sun & Moon Classics: 112 / American Theater in Literature)
ISBN: 1-55713-228-3 (acid-free paper)
1. Dracula, Count (Fictitious character)—Drama.. 2. Vampires—Drama.
I. Title. II. Series.
PS3573.E468L36 1995
812'.54—dc20
95-25658
CIP

Printed in the United States of America on acid-free paper.

Without limiting the rights under copyright reserved here,
no part of this publication may be reproduced, stored in or introduced into
a retrieval system, or transmitted, in any form or by any means
(electronic, mechanical, photocopying, recording or otherwise),
without the prior written permission of both the copyright owner
and the above publisher of the book.

Contents

Dracula

– 7 –

Swoop

– 65 –

Dracula

Dracula premiered at the SoHo Repertory Theatre in New York, April 1994, with the following cast:

MINA	Patricia Dunnock
LUCY	Julia Gibson
JONATHAN HARKER	Tim Blake Nelson
DRACULA	Thomas Jay Ryan
NUN	Sharon Brady
DR. SEWARD	Damian Young
VAN HELSING	Ray Xifo
SIMMONS	Christopher McCann
QUINCEY MORRIS	Brett Rickaby
VAMPYRETTE	Gloria Domination
VAMPYRETTE	Jackie Domination
VAMPYRETTE	Marti Domination

Directed by Julian Webber. Set Design: Kyle Chepulis. Lighting Design: Brian Aldous. Costume Design: James Sauli. Sound Design: John Kilgore. Casting: Peggy Adler. Original Music: Melissa Shiflett. Assistant Director: Jason Porath.

The action takes place in the last days of 1899.

*

Note: The occasional appearance of an asterisk in the middle of a speech indicates that the next speech begins to overlap at that point. A double asterisk indicates that a later speech (not the one immediately following) begins to overlap at that point. The overlapping speeches are all clearly marked in the text.

Act One

A world of decaying and unlikely machinery. Big glass tubes with things crawling in them. Huge light bulbs that flicker. Strange tubes that lead everywhere. Water stains down black walls.

Door slam.

Pin spot on a face, pale and drained...

MINA: The room was dark. The bed was empty. I lit a match and found she was not there. The door was shut but not locked as I had left it. "Thank God," I said to myself, "She cannot be far, as she is only in her nightdress." I ran downstairs and looked in the sitting room. Finally I came to the hall door and found it open. It was not wide-open, but the catch of the lock had not caught. Lucy must have gone out as she was.

Music.

I took a big, heavy shawl and ran after. There was a bright, full moon, with dense, black, driving clouds, and the clock was striking one as I arrived at the Crescent. Not a soul was in sight. I ran along the North Terrace, but could see no sign of the white figure I expected. The entire harbor of Whitby lay beneath me, and the glistening sea beyond. At the edge of the West Cliff above the pier I looked across the harbor to the East Cliff, in hope or fear—I don't know which—of seeing Lucy at our favorite seat overlooking the town. For a moment or two I could see nothing, as the shadow of a cloud obscured St. Mary's Church and all around it. Then, as the cloud passed, I could see, there, just as I had expected, the silver light of the moon strike a half reclining figure, snowy white. But it seemed to me as though something dark stood behind the seat, and bent over it.

What it was, whether man or beast, I could not tell; I did not wait to catch another glance, but flew down the steep steps to the pier and along by Gin Lane and the fish market to the bridge, which was the only way to reach the East Cliff. The town seemed dead, for not a soul did I see. That was good. For Lucy's reputation was at stake. My knees trembled, and my breath labored as I toiled up the endless steps. When I got to the top I could see the seat and the white figure. There was undoubtedly something long and black bending over her. Lucy! Lucy! Something raised its head. For a minute or so I lost sight of her. When I came into view again the cloud had passed, and the moonlight struck so brilliantly that I could see Lucy, quite distinctly, her head lying over the back of the seat. She was quite alone.

Dracula 13

A bright light on the other side of the theater,
LUCY *appears.*

LUCY: It all seemed quite real, for I knew I was not
dreaming. I only wanted to be at this particular
spot—I don't know why, for I was afraid of something—I don't know what. I do know I wanted to
do something; something very, very bad. I remember, though I suppose I was asleep, passing
through the streets and over the bridge. A fish
leaped as I passed by. And I heard a lot of dogs
barking and howling, all barking at once, as I went
up the steps. Then I had a vague memory of something long and dark with red eyes; and something
very sweet and very bitter all around me at once;
and then I seemed to be sinking into deep green
water, and there was a singing in my ears, as I
have heard there is to drowning men. My soul
seemed to go out from my body and float about
in the air. I seem to remember that, for a time,
the West lighthouse was underneath, as if I had
been thrown into the air. All I wanted was to be
with you and Jack and Quincy and dear Professor Van Helsing. And then I came back and found
you shaking my body. I saw you do it before I felt
you.

Lighting change and calliope. Seaside at Whitby.
LUCY *and* MINA *on a balcony.*

MINA: Strange. This particular night has put me in
mind of poor Jonathan, and the journal of his

last, sad, strange, business trip to the land beyond the forest....

LUCY: To the land beyond the forest? Whatever land
beyond the forest do you mean?

MINA: You know which land, Lucy.

LUCY: Why don't you simply say Transylvania and be
done with it?

MINA: Lucy, you are so fractious since we arrived in
Whitby, and your behavior in general has caused
me no little vexation.

LUCY: Mina, must you dwell on morbid matters?
Whitby is such a pleasant seaside town, if only
you would let yourself enjoy it. The harbor is quite
colorful, full of curious folk and quaint pleasures.
It is our holiday, after all.

MINA: Lucy, how can you be so tactless?

LUCY: Forgive me, Mina. I don't wish to hurt you, really. It is only that I worry about you. Why must
we be forever retelling the same old tale, as if the
retelling of it might ease your torment?

Music, lights, Transylvania.
She reads as JONATHAN *appears behind a scrim,*
seated. A strange COACHMAN *stands by.*

JONATHAN: ...we were leaving the West and entering
the East...

COACHMAN: Budapesth

JONATHAN: Budapesth seems a wonderful place. We
viewed the ruins of...

COACHMAN: Klausenburgh.

JONATHAN: The Hotel Royale. I had for supper a
chicken done up some way with red pepper, which

Dracula   15

was very good, but thirsty. Memo. Get recipe for Mina. After supper a very unusual entertainment.

Curtains open. Music / Puppet Show.

*

DRACULA: Listen, my dear, to the children of the night.

GIRL: Why may I not go this evening?

DRACULA: Because, my dear, my coachman and horse are away on business.

GIRL: But I would walk with pleasure.

DRACULA: And your baggage?

GIRL: I do not care about it. I want to get away at once.

He lunges at her.

Oh, oh, my God. He has placed his reeking lip upon my throat and bitten me!

Attacks DRACULA with a mallet.

*

Music/Puppet Show Out.

JONATHAN: I have read that every known superstition is gathered up in the horseshoe of the Carpathians. Memo. Must ask the Count about these. I had for breakfast more paprika and a sort of porridge of maize flour which they said was "mamaliga…"

COACHMAN: Mamaliga… [*correcting pronunciation*]

16   MAC WELLMAN

JONATHAN: ...and eggplant stuffed with forcemeat,
    which they call "implemata"...
COACHMAN: Implemata... [*correcting pronunciation*]
JONATHAN: Memo. Get recipe for this also.
    Hhhquulptu.
COACHMAN: Bukovina.
JONATHAN: At Bukovina bit of a tumble with a pretty
    fille de chambre at the Golden Krone Hotel...
COACHMAN: Bistritz
JONATHAN: At Bistritz I dined on what they call
    "Robber's steak," chunks of bacon, onion, and
    beef, seasoned with red pepper, and strung on
    sticks and roasted over the fire, in the simple style
    of London's cat's meat.
OLD WOMAN: [*the following in Romanian*] It is now
    the Eve of St. George's Day. Do you not know
    that tonight when the clock strikes midnight, all
    evil things in the world have full sway? Do you
    know where you are going, and what you are go-
    ing to?
JONATHAN: The wine was golden Mediasch, which
    produces a queer sting on the tongue, which is,
    however, not disagreeable.

    The OLD WOMAN *turns, puts a crucifix around
    his neck and exits crossing herself. Turns back.*

OLD WOMAN: For your mother's sake.
JONATHAN: I had only a couple of glasses of this, and
    nothing else.

    The OLD WOMAN *exits. We hear peasants mut-
    tering.*

Dracula

JONATHAN: I could hear a lot of words, repeated. Queer words. I quietly got my polyglot dictionary from my bag and looked them out. I must say they were not cheering to me. Ordog (Satan), Pokol (Hell), Stregoica (witch), Vrolok Vlkoslak, both of which mean the same thing; one being Slovak and the other Servian for something that is either werewolf or vampire.

COACHMAN: Borgo Pass.

JONATHAN: Memo. Must ask the Count why these superstitions persist.

> JONATHAN *exits coach scrim and nervously enters.* DRACULA *opens curtain wearing an apron. A roast chicken on a platter.*

DRACULA: Because your peasant is at heart a coward and a fool. It is said, for instance, that blue flames, the fire of St.George's Eve, appear on one night, and on that night no man of this land will, if he can help it, leave his house. This and other idiotic legend. Harmless.

JONATHAN: I agree.

DRACULA: Possible to find much red gold where the blue flame dances. Treasure of olden days. We are in Transylvania, and Transylvania is not England.

JONATHAN: There you are right.

DRACULA: I am *Boyar,* the common people know me and I am master.

JONATHAN: There you are most certainly right.

DRACULA: I have studied all our correspondence. Come, tell me of England and of the house you have procured for me there.

JONATHAN: A bottle of old Tokay! How wonderful!

DRACULA: The house.

JONATHAN: The estate is called "Carfax." Surrounded by a big wall. Built of heavy stones. The gates are of oak and iron. Massive. All eaten by rust, however. It has not been repaired for years. Solid, Gothic, solemn. There is a deep, dark-looking pond which makes it gloomy. Third Mortgage. Easy terms. Next door is a private lunatic asylum. Run by an old acquaintance, a friend of my wife, Mina. His name is Jack Seward. In fact, he courted her before I, the dog. Unsuccessfully, of course.

DRACULA: I am glad that it is old and big. We Transylvanian nobles love not to think our bones may lie among the common lot. I seek not gaiety, nor mirth, nor the bright voluptuousness of much sunshine and sparkling waters, which please the young and gay. I am no longer young; and my heart, through weary years of mourning over the dead, is not attuned to mirth. I love the shadow and the shade and would be alone with my thoughts when I may.

He begins to leave.

JONATHAN: Somehow his words and looks did not seem in accord.

DRACULA: By the bye, I advise you not to leave your room at night, otherwise I cannot vouch for your safety.

Dracula   19

He closes the curtain. Blackout. JONATHAN *appears around curtain in spot.*

JONATHAN: But I escaped before he could do his wicked thing to me. Xxlld. Fpfptssc. So lovely there, we and the deadly.

NUNS *chant.*

I love Lucy. Kcm. Kcm. Bats. Bats. Interference from the future. Red dogs. Nuns. Goop. Magic lanterns. They warned me, they did. Can't say I wasn't warned. All in the diaries, all of it. He's going to England. Fresh blood. Needs it. Carfax. Large old stones. Easy terms. Qqqmc. Mina must learn to keep a proper diary. It's a horror. Like the movies. What's a movie? Moving world. Yes, desperation. Bonka bonka bonka bonk. And oh, the terrible twitching bag. The poor mother torn to pieces by hundreds of wolves in the awful courtyard.

NUN *starts to speak.*

Unspeakable. Xxxuuma. Fancy *him* at the British museum, as a sort of tourist! Looking at the Rosetta stone! Bat. Baseball bat. What in the name of heaven's that? Ah, the precious flask of slivovitz. I am a radio. What's a radio?

Insane laughter.

The milk that is spilt cries out not afterwards. A dog-eared diary, with real dog ears. I'd as soon eat molecules with chopsticks as dine with Count Deville. Dvlmnoa. Oao. Truly, the mad cause one to doubt the plan of God. Ha ha. He shall enter, yes, like those horrid bulls. Bonka bonk. Judge Moneybag will solve this. Beware the puppet show. The Black Dog shall land at Whitby by the North Sea. With his dirt. In big boxes. O. Then to downtown Whitby. Kkfffxxo. Get ye hammers and a spike. Oh, the diaries are so important! "What took it out?" What bloody well took it out indeed! Aye, there's the crux. O, a, u, O, a, u. X all the way to X' and half the alcohol. X all the way to the walking fruit stand that is the Lord Mayor of Popinjay. X all the way to Kfx. Peppercorn in my pocket, and, oh, my mind's on fire. Flies, spiders, sparrows, cats. Peach Bottom reactor full of sleepers, o, a, u. He shall slide under the sash and stand before me, as the moon does in all her glory.

NUN: Madam, he has been like this since he was found by Gypsies wandering about in the Borgo Pass, leaping from tussock to tussock, raving about blood and wolves and the lord knows what. He has suffered from a terrible brain seizure. It appears now that he will survive, but unfortunately his wits may be a trifle impaired. Permanently. Unless heavily sedated he goes on in this fashion interminably. He calls himself "Scardanelli" and remembers nothing of his former life. Which is why it took us so long, with the aid of merciful

Dracula 21

God, to locate his loved ones. He was very thin and pale when we found him. Truly, the torments of the mad almost make one doubt the plan of God.

She tears off her habit, throws it down and tramples on it.

MINA: What could have produced such a violent effect on poor Jonathan?

Insane burlesque music.
Flashback to Castle Dracula. 3 VAMPYRETTES *appear. They dance. They approach, closer.*

VAMPYRETTE 1: Who is to be the first?

VAMPYRETTE 2: Hush, silly, there are kisses for all.

DRACULA: How dare you disobey me? I warned you, he is mine. You shall have him only when I am done.

VAMPYRETTE 2: Just as at Cassovo! Why should we believe him? He will betray one of us to our enemies.

VAMPYRETTE 1: You, you never loved.

DRACULA: You know how well I have loved.

VAMPYRETTE 2: You said you loved Theodora, then you gave her to the Turks.

VAMPYRETTE 3: And she loved you so.

DRACULA: Be quiet, fools. Remember the Woiwode Stephen was my brother.

VAMPYRETTE 3: All these centuries, and you still treat the fine ladies who serve you with contempt.

DRACULA: Be gone. Or you shall feel my wrath.
VAMPYRETTE 1: Are we to have nothing?

> *Jiggling bag. Baby crying. They pause and seize it.*
>
> *Blackout. Lights up on the raving* JONATHAN / SCARDANELLI *as before. Now* SEWARD *has joined* MINA.

MINA: Dear Jack, what kind of sickness is this? Sucked dry as a prune, with his poor wits wandering like the fabled antipodes of St. Viar. Oh, Jonathan, poor Jonathan. Why doesn't he recognize me?
SEWARD: Mina, it was wise of you to bring him here. Especially in view of our longstanding association. My asylum is the most up-to-date in this part of the country. My, your perfume makes me heady. I always was susceptible to odors, particularly female odors. No, this resembles some kind of absolute, bestial possession. As if—my God— the poor fellow has been terrified out of his right mind by some apparitional, but nevertheless, fully convincing monstrosity. It happens, especially when there is congenital weakness of the personality sructure.* As I recall being the case with Jonathan.
MINA: What on earth do you mean by a "congenital weakness of the personality structure?"
SEWARD: Let us be frank with one another, Mina. Jonathan always was an odd duck.
MINA: But what can be done?
SEWARD: I know of only one man who can help us.

Dracula   23

He is an alienist and specialist of obscure mala-
dies. My professor at Leiden in fact. Van Helsing
is his name. Without my assistance his renowned
Atlas of a Rat's Brain simply would not have been
possible.*

MINA: Science is making truly remarkable advances
these days.

SEWARD: He resides at Amsterdam, and owing to a
peculiar and private disability of an unmention-
able sort is reluctant to travel.

MINA: Oh dear...

She departs, he doesn't notice.

SEWARD: But that's another matter. But, perhaps, in
this case, I may be able to prevail upon him. My
your perfume has the queerest effect on me. I do
think I had better sit down.

VAN HELSING: Let me tell you my friend that there
are things done today in electrical science which
would have been deemed unholy by the very men
who discovered electricity.

He enters.

There are mysteries in life. Why was it
Methusalah lived nine hundred years? Can you
tell why, why, when other spiders die small and
soon, that one great spider lived centuries in the
tower of the old Spanish church and grew and
grew till, on descending, he drank the oil out of
all the church lamps?

SEWARD: Whatever are you driving at?

VAN HELSING: From your letter, I surmise his may be a special case. May I become level with you Jack? I am partially overcome my old fear of strange beds to come here. Who knows? Maybe I can decipher ancient mystery. Show me the poor man.

> SEWARD *whistles.* SIMMONS *brings* JONATHAN.
> VAN HELSING *examines* JONATHAN.

VAN HELSING: Jack, my friend. I am glad you call. This is not, I fear, normal mad. But unnatural one. Possession by dark forces of the forest. A virus of the undead. All signs indicate such. Vacant eye, like an empty wallet. Preposterous talk of wolf. Loss of memory of previous life: name, wife, solicitor's trade. A complete big blank. Instead, ridiculous new name, "Scardanelli." Sudden abomination of garlic and spicy food. Insectivore habit. Have been bitten. Chewed about the throat. Mosquito bite? No, no, Jack.

SEWARD: Professor, let me be your student again. I feel like a madman lumbering through a bog in a mist, jumping from one tussock to another, in the mere blind effort to move without knowing where I am going.

VAN HELSING: Good image.

> *Whistle.* JONATHAN *is removed.*

My thesis is that I want you to believe.

SEWARD: To believe what?

Dracula

VAN HELSING: To believe things that cannot.

SEWARD: Then you want me not to let some previous conviction injure the receptivity of my mind regarding some strange matter. Do I read your lesson right?

VAN HELSING: Is Wampyr.

SEWARD: What?

VAN HELSING: But not chewed enough to become undead self. No, but is work of Wampyr.

SEWARD: What's that in God's name?

Music.

VAN HELSING: Wampyr. Is undead. Blood sucking mysterium. Inexplicable hocus-pocus. An abomination. Have read big, old tomes on such. In black mountains of Transylvania drunk Gypsy dance around the wooden red dog and shout horrible. *Ordog ordog ordog ordog vlkoslak!* Rage in blood. Tell tale of aristocrat *Boyar* warrior clan who fight Turk with strange mud pies, flying door jambs, boiling slime from wizard pot. Something go wrong in alchemical concoction. Instead of normal necromancy a change happen to this certain nobleman. He become an effigy of marble smooth—white, blood-eating, invulnerable to storm, cross-bow, or musket. Undead be born. Virus cannot be traced to rotten meat, obscene sexual rite of autumnal haystack, nor the French itch. Maybe the devil have made this devil thing.

SEWARD: What must we do?

VAN HELSING: I am not prepare to say. Employ sci-

entific method and hope for best. I have bought
bottle of *Oude Genever*. Care for nightcap?
Wampyr can wait.

He exits. SEWARD *whistles. Summons*
SIMMONS *who brings chloral.* SEWARD *takes*
some and leans back in drugged reverie.

SEWARD: Chloral, the modern Morpheus! I must be
careful not to let it be a habit. But I am weary
and low in spirits tonight. Perhaps all my research
into the human brain has been for nothing. The
expeditions to Peru, Tangiers, Mbululand. I am
tired of everyone. This damnable itch to reason
it all out, and be impartial. To judge what is sane,
and what is not. When all I want to do is leap
from the top of St. Mary's and flap to my death
shrieking my hatred for all of them. Lucy who
would not have me, and Mina who would not
have me. And who both tempt me. As for the secret to mortal reason and mortal desire, how many
brain smears have I examined and not found it?
And our poor damned "Scardanelli" says his God
is near, but difficult to grasp. When everyone
knows that God is far away and lives in the sky.
There is no limit to mortal aggravation.

Music, VAMPYRETTES *in the sky packing gear*
into suitcases.
Lighting change. Bird sounds. MINA *strides in.*

MINA: When Jonathan recovers the use of his facili-

Dracula   27

ties I shall be able to be very useful to him, and if I can stenograph well enough I can take down what he wants to say in this way and write it out for him on the typewriter, at which I am also practicing very hard.

LUCY: Mina, we have told all our secrets to each other since we were children. We have slept together and eaten together and laughed and cried together. And so now, Mina. Can't you guess? Oh, Mina, I love him. And him. And him.

Lighting separately on SEWARD, VAN HELSING *and* QUINCEY MORRIS.

Well, my dear, number one came before lunch. Doctor Jack Seward, with the strong jaw and the good forehead. You know him, I believe. He was very cool outwardly…

SEWARD: Lucy, will you marry me?

LUCY: But he kept playing with a scalpel in a way that nearly made me scream! Just fancy! He is only nine and twenty and he has an immense lunatic asylum all under his care.* Number two is Quincey Morris. He is an American with such a sweet accent, who has become frightfully rich importing scrap metal to Japan and Winchesters to Latin America.

MINA: Yes, he always did play with a scalpel. Oh, go on.

QUINCEY: Lucy, will you marry me?

LUCY: And sweet old Professor Van Helsing who has been consulting with Jack on some strange matter. So stable and strong…

28   MAC WELLMAN

VAN HELSING: Lucy, will you marry me?

LUCY: Poor man, his wife lies in a coma near Amsterdam, a complete vegetable, due to a faulty innoculation during the recent outbreak of cholera in the Low countries. Does that make his courting of me bigamy?

MINA: It seems so important to keep a record of things. There is so little to hold on to otherwise. It all flies up the chimney. And what with Jonathan in the queer state he is in. I don't know what else to do. You might as well know, it is Jack's hospital where Jonathan is sequestered. And what with my weak stomach and all, Jack has* absolutely forbade me from seeing him.

LUCY: You know what I did? I told Doctor Seward I would not have him, but would have Quincey Morris instead. It was a fib, for I am very fond of Jack. But I was curious to see what he would do. He blushed and his ears moved up and down ever so slightly. Then he gave out with the most curious moan. I know what you're thinking, Mina: why are men so noble when women are so little worthy of them?

JONATHAN *enters pursued by* SIMMONS.

JONATHAN: I know what you are thinking, Doctor Seward. "A strange and sudden change in Scardanelli last night." You have noticed, haven't you? I began to get excited and sniff about like a dog. Your man Simmons, the lecher, was struck by my manner and, knowing your interest in me,

Dracula   29

encouraged me to talk. I am usually respectful to servants. Even to him. Sometimes I am positively obsequious. But last night all I could say was: "I don't want to talk to you. The Master is at hand."

SEWARD: [*in a sudden rage*] What!? You don't mean to tell me that you don't care about spiders anymore?

JONATHAN: Bother them all! I don't care a pin about them.

SEWARD: You are too dangerous to be roaming about. Up to now your hobby has been catching flies. You have had such a number I have had myself to expostulate. Then you turn your mind to spiders. You have got several big fellows in a box. You feed them with flies, I know. Soon your spiders are as great a nuisance as your flies. I say you must clear out some of these. You apparently acquiesce, cheerfully. Then a horrid blowfly, bloated with some carrion food, buzzes into the room. You catch it, hold it exultantly for a few minutes between thumb and forefinger, and then before I know what to do, you put it into your mouth and eat it.

JONATHAN: It was very good and wholesome. It was life, strong life. Life gives life.

SEWARD: Then the tame sparrow incident

JONATHAN: I tamed the sparrow by feeding it with spiders. And flies.

SEWARD: Quite. That is the crux.

JONATHAN: My flies are considerably diminished as you yourself requested, Doctor.

SEWARD: Quite so. Indeed you grow more interesting every day.

JONATHAN: But my sparrow is gone. It's flown away. But a kitten! A nice, little, sleek, playful kitten. That is what I want. That I can play with, and teach, and feed and feed and feed and feed.

SEWARD: The thought that has been buzzing about in my mind lately is complete, and the theory proved. My maniac is of a peculiar kind. I shall have to invent a new classification for you. You are a zoophagous maniac.

JONATHAN: What the devil does "zoophagous" mean?

SEWARD: It means *life-eating,* you fiend. And what you desire is to absorb as many lives as you can, and you are scheming a plan to achieve this in a cumulative way. You give many flies to one spider, and many spiders to one sparrow, and now you want a cat to feed the sparrow to. BUT YOU YOURSELF HAVE EATEN THE SPAR-ROW!

Slaps JONATHAN *on the back: feathers.*

Men sneered at vivisection, and yet look at it's results today! Why not develop science in its most difficult and vital aspect—the knowledge of the brain?

JONATHAN: Shut up, Doctor. The Master is coming.

SEWARD: Had I the secret of even one such mind— the key to the fancy of one such lunatic—I might advance my own branch of science to a pitch compared with which Burton-Sanderson's physiology of Ferrier's brain knowledge would be as nothing.

Dracula 31

JONATHAN: Envy is a crippling affliction, Dr. Seward, and your obsession with brain-matter smacks of rank determinism.

SEWARD: What would you know of these higher things? I do believe one day I shall locate the spot, the very lobe, governing sexual license, which may, by application of the galvanic charge, be rendered inoperable, giving us some peace at night.

JONATHAN: I only asked for a kitten.

SEWARD: Ah, Lucy, how I wish you had forgiven me, for that day I spilled myself on your pretty pink skirt. It was beyond nature to control myself. Oh, Lucy, Lucy, though I have sat upon and crushed my hat I cannot be angry with you, nor can I be angry with my friend, Quincey Morris, that American ape, whose happiness is yours; but I must only wait on, hopeless. And work. And try not to think of you and him. In a little room at that inn. By the Aerated Bread Company. Your favorite satins. Lilac and the odor of your...and you and him, like beasts, at it. Work! And work!

JONATHAN: What about my kitten?

SEWARD: You shall not have a cat, you shall have an opiate.

Whistles.

Simmons, prepare an opiate for "Scardanelli," a powerful opiate. We must get to the bottom of this "Wampyr" business.

SIMMONS *administers opiate.* JONATHAN *becomes strange.*

JONATHAN: I am here to do your bidding, Master. I am your slave, and you will reward me, for I shall be faithful. I have worshipped you long and far off. Now that you are near, I await your commands, and you will not pass me by, will you dear Master, in your distribution of good things.

> JONATHAN *collapses.* SIMMONS *bears him off.*
> *Music*
> *Song.* SIMMONS *entertains* LUCY *with a song.*

> Simmon's Song

> We all go down to the sea,
> and do there secretly
> What we crave in the dark.
> Bonka, bonka, bonka, bonk.

> LUCY *appears on her seat on the East Cliff.*

> Mad Sally has me in her mouth.
> Bonka, bonka, bonka, bonk.
> Bonka, bonka, bonka, bonk. etc.

SIMMONS: That's the song old man Swales used to sing. The oldest loony in the place. It's the bovine warble to his voice as does it. Face like the arsehole of that rhinosteros I seen at the carny near the Black Dog. A bloomin bewhiskered pine-

Dracula
33

apple. Banished from the Royal Navy he was, I hear tell, for sodomizing a cabin boy with a bloody belayin' pin, right smack in the old Adriatic. Them as knows, knows. Look, look, there's something in that wind that tastes like death. It's in the air, I feel it comin'.

Looking grim.

That ship there, from Eastern Europe, by the look of her. She's knockin' about in the queerest way. As if no one's aboard. Alive, that is.

Gettin' late Miss Lucy, I'd best be back to the nut-house or the loonies'll have Master Jack climbin' the bloody walls. They rattle 'im, they do. If it weren't for me, they'd rattle 'im worse, I expect. What's more? The pay stinks.

Exit.
Seaside sound effects. MINA *enters in a rush with a discovery: a book. She hands it to* LUCY.

LUCY: From the log of the freighter "Demeter." On 6 July we finish taking on cargo. Boxes of earth, four in all. Transport consigned to Whitby, England.

Sea sound changes to screaking ship.

On 11 July at dawn entered the Bosporus. Backsheesh.

MINA: [*interrupting*] That's a bribe.

LUCY: On 13 July passed Cape Matapan. Crew dissatisfied about something. Scared, but would not speak out.

On 14 July anxious about crew. Men all steady fellows. Mate could not tell what was wrong. They only told him there was *something* and crossed themselves.

On 16 July one of the crew, Petrofsky, is missing. Men say there is *something* aboard.

17 July. Olgaren says to me he saw a tall thin man who was not like any of the crew, come up the companion-way and go along the deck forward, and disappear. Searched the ship. Nothing.

24 July. Another man lost.

29 July. Another tragedy. Krupa gone.

30 July. Only self and mate left.

1 August. At midnight, I went to relieve the man at the wheel, and when I got to it found no one there.

4 August. Still fog, which sunlight cannot pierce. I am alone, and in the dimness of the night I saw it—him!

Last page ripped and bloody. Screams as ship sounds out. Pause. Sea background sound effect.

And if we are wrecked mayhap this bottle may be found and those who find it understand...

Meanwhile a dog appears carrying suitcase.

Dracula   35

MINA: How very strange! An immense dog has leapt
from the wreck, there on the beach. My, what a
remarkably large and attractive dog. Where do
you suppose such a great brute beast came from,
and who do you suppose will feed him?

LUCY *gets sleepy.*

You seemed so tired, Lucy. I like to watch you
when you sleep. Some of the "new women" writ-
ers will one day start an idea that men and women
should be allowed to see each other asleep before proposing or accepting.

*She freezes in pose. Lighting change and cal-
liope. And drip.*
VAMPYRETTES *enter seaside waxworks to view*
MINA, LUCY *and* VAN HELSING *and* SEWARD *in
scrim poses.*

VAMPYRETTES: [*mocking her*] Poor Lucy, I suppose
she will be sleepwalking again. Then tomorrow
she will be drained. A brave man's blood is the
best thing when a woman is in trouble. All this
puts me in a brown study, and I think of poor
Jonathan, sucked dry as a puckered flatworm.
Poor crazy "Scardanelli"! I believe I shall require
an opiate.

They exit. Pause. VAN HELSING *and* SEWARD
in secret conference. They look around.

36 MAC WELLMAN

VAN HELSING: This Dracula know me as sheep known by lamb-chop man. I going to extirpate malign of cancer wampyr. Drive stake through grisly undead heart. Garlic in mouth after chop off head. Hard work. Need saw. Chain. Hammer. Rope. Work table. Wampyr have cunning brain, but child brain. As for instance, of monkey with hand in cookie jar. Ha. Dracula now in England. How do I know? Examine raving "zoophagous" patient "Scardanelli," formerly normally respectable one Jonathan Harker. He engaged to find house for Count Deville, alias Dracula. He have, so to say, telegraph wire to primordial will of our wampyr.

SEWARD: You mean this wampyr is in England?

VAN HELSING: Here. There. Maybe even in Whitby where we stand. Manifest of undead ship "Demeter." Four boxes of grim, fine-mashed Carpathian mould. Of what use to England? Make sand castle? No. Is bed of wampyr. Nice, cozy earth smell. Kinda dig into and relax. Do inert wampyr business. At dawn wampyr must sleep. All these boxes are sent to old house. Somewhere unclear from soggy manifest.

SEWARD: Simmons! He works the docks on his days off. He might know where the boxes were delivered.

MINA: [*clatters in*] Jack, if you don't mind. All this commotion. My stomach. Don't you think I could have just a little?

SEWARD: Be quiet, Mina. If we are to get to the bottom of this strange business which for your own protection you must know nothing about, we must have absolute discipline.

Dracula 37

VAN HELSING: Give her the medication, John.

He gives her chloral, and she retires discreetly to take it.

Poor Lucy have all signs too. Watch for unnecessary foreigner with biting habit. On throat vein. Find and destroy the undead pest. Before further harm. Squalor of harbor slum make good home for *Nosferatu*. Where do we find your assistant?

Lighting and sound effects for pub.

SEWARD: He's probably in there. The notorious Black Dog tavern.

Two VAMPYRETTES *emerge.* SEWARD *goes into pub discombobulated.*

VAMPYRETTES: A moment of silence for poor Jonathan.

They exit pursued by a suspicious VAN HELSING. SEWARD *drags* SIMMONS *from pub.*

SIMMONS: Well Guv'nor, I forgits, but it was empty.
SEWARD: How did you get into the house if it was empty?
SIMMONS: The old gent that engaged me opened up. Curse me but he was the strongest chap I ever struck. Why, 'e took up 'is end o' the boxes like they was pounds of tea...

38   MAC WELLMAN

SEWARD: Just shut up and tell me the number of the
    house.
SIMMONS: What with all the beer, I can hardly re-
    member the county.

        SEWARD *throws him down.*

SEWARD: A total waste of time.

        LUCY'S *seat high over Whitby on the East Ter-
        race.* DRACULA *appears.*

LUCY: Count Deville, you are quite the most experi-
    enced man I have ever met. Quincey is sweet.
    You don't know Quincey, but he is sweet. In the
    American way, with great, earnest quacks and
    gulps. Cows' eyes. Marmalade, really. Odd, I can't
    imagine him undressed. Though I cannot help
    but imagine Simmons that way. Jack's man,
    Simmons? Big, round, stiff Simmons. My, you
    are the smoothest gentleman. I hear the ladies of
    Paris are pretty and saucy. Do you think I am
    impertinent, my dear Count? You may call me
    Ishtar if you like. Bobo calls me that. Pity my
    friends aren't more sophisticated. We could all
    go for an outing over the wold, or have a glorious
    dinner party. However, they lack *savoir faire.* But
    today they're all down to Whitby harbor on some
    queer business. A place filled with immoral back
    alleys. Gin Lane. The Black Dog tavern. It is
    strange. The man always finds the girl alone.

        Pause.

Dracula

I feel a curious tingle when I am with you, Count Deville. Lizst does that to me also. What a fine, hairy man you are—even the palms of your hands. I am a silly girl, aren't I? Who could imagine a big, long man of your vast experience interested in a silly slip of a thing like me?

DRACULA: Quite the contrary.

Music.
Kisses her.

LUCY: Do it again.

Kisses her.

I won't tell. Whatever happens.

Kisses her again.

Oh, that's a darker kind of sweetness. But I like it, I really do. Oh, but there isn't much time, so you must do it all now, because no one must discover us together. Mina would throw up. Oh, I won't tell anyone, but you must show me what to do and how...

Bites her.

Oh my...

Bites her and sucks.

Oh, this is how it is.

Pause.

I'm bleeding a little, is that all right?

Pause.

I think I am very fond of you.

Back to the Black Dog, only now we're inside. SIMMONS *and* SEWARD *drinking.*

SIMMONS: Do you recall the old days at the Fortress at Mbululand? The native girls with their long, naked legs, and spent three-ten Greener cartridges tied up in their hair?
SEWARD: Oh do shut up, for God's sake, Simmons.

Oompah music.

SIMMONS: Remember how we used to go at it high in the Andean Sierra? Panpipes and the young Indian girls. Busy at both ends of that fine, strapping one, eh Master Jack? Bonka, bonka, bonk.
SEWARD: Simmons, you do recall the queerest things, after all.

More bad music and general vulgarity.

SIMMONS: Don't suppose you recall the stews of Tangiers? Oh, pretend you don't. The swish of silk and the tinkle of little silver bells about the ankles of little girls. Bonka, bonka, bonka, bonk Shshshshshsh.

Dracula 41

Curtains open with fanfare as VAMPYRETTES *perform dirty poem on infernal fucking machine. Total tasteless pandemonium. Everyone running. Whistler blows as* VAN HELSING *enters.*

VAN HELSING: Lucy is ill; that is, she has no special disease, but she looks awful, and is getting worse. I fear it is you know what. Wampyr.
SEWARD: My God! This is dreadful. There is no time to be lost. She will die from sheer want of blood.
VAN HELSING: There must be a transfusion of blood.

They attach LUCY *to infernal transfusion machine.*

SEWARD: I am younger and stronger, professor. It must be me.
VAN HELSING: Then get ready at once. I have my bag. I must prepare.

As they set up QUINCEY *enters.*

QUINCEY: Lucy's in a bad fix, I hear from Simmons.
VAN HELSING: Sir, you are in time. You are the lover of our dear miss. She is bad; very, very bad.
QUINCEY: What can I do? I'd give the last drop of my blood to save her.

At this SEWARD *becomes downcast.*

VAN HELSING: You are a man, and it is a man that we want.
LUCY: [*sitting up*] What's the matter with me anyhow?

42 MAC WELLMAN

VAN HELSING *mixes a narcotic for her.*

VAN HELSING: Now little miss, here is your medicine. Drink it off, like good child. See, I lift you so that to swallow is easy.

Forces it down her throat.

VAN HELSING: You (Quincey) may take that one little kiss while I bring over the table. Friend John, help me.

They lower transfusion table. Pause as QUINCEY *considers his love.*

QUINCEY: If only you knew how gladly I would die for her.
VAN HELSING: Good boy.

Stabs him with a needle. They lie him down and exit.

MINA: Jack, if you don't mind. My stomach?

SEWARD *takes chloral and staggers out into the hallway after* MINA.
Lighting change. The transfusion continues.

QUINCEY: Miss Lucy, I know I ain't good enough to regulate the fixin's of your little shoes. Won't you just hitch alongside of me and let us go down the long road together, driving in double harness?

Dracula 43

LUCY: I don't know anything of hitching and such. And frankly, I find your interest in my shoes in somewhat bad taste. And as for the long road, I'm not yet broken to harness. But I'm eager to try...

He passes out for lack of blood.

Shall we meet tonight behind the Black Dog Tavern? That's where, so I hear, the poor girls go when the heat seizes. But you mustn't tell a soul. Promise?

Sees he's passed out.

Quincey, sometimes you are the very cipher of a man.

Lighting up on SEWARD *and* MINA. *They clinch.* SEWARD *does something unforgiveable. He runs away.* MINA *follows.*

MINA: Jack, may I ask for a special favor? I was wondering if I might see him again. Even if there's little hope. My stomach is feeling a bit more stable now. It's just that I must know more of his condition.

SEWARD: There has been little change.

MINA: Just once more...

SEWARD: He refers to himself as "Scardanelli," and says he possesses a master who is God and is near but difficult to grasp. Eats flies. Feeds them to spiders. Ate a bird once. A nice, little sparrow that never hurt anyone. Another time he attacked me with a chair. I suffered a wound, here, upon the arm. It bled. Before that idiot Simmons could restrain him, he was on all fours lapping up blood like a kitten. Quite batty. His linen is most rank. Very well. It's not as if he's been kept prisoner,

He winches open JONATHAN'S *cell door.*

A lady would like to speak with you.

JONATHAN: Oh, very well, let her come in, by all means. But wait just a minute till I tidy the place up.

Eats all the flies and spiders, flypaper, etc.

Let the lady come in.

MINA: Good evening, Mr. Scardanelli.

JONATHAN: You're not the girl the doctor wanted to marry, are you? You can't be, you know, for she is very ill.

MINA: Oh no! I have a husband of my own. I am Mrs. Harker. Do you remember Jonathan Harker?

JONATHAN: Ah, it was your husband, poor Jonathan, who was sucked as dry as a parched cerement in the land beyond the forest.

MINA: We have had no word from my husband for some time now. But we would like to know where he is.

Dracula   45

JONATHAN: Then what are you doing here?

MINA: [*laugh*] I am staying on a visit with Miss Lucy
Westenra

JONATHAN: Don't stay. For the master is near and at
hand.

MINA: We must find your master, for he has taken the
soul of my dear husband whose acquaintance you
have surely made. You must surely recall the name
Jonathan Harker.

JONATHAN: Ah, yes, his father was the inventor of a
burnt rum punch much favored on Derby Day.
All they serve me here is "mamaliga."

MINA: Do you recall the name Jonathan Harker? You
must try* very hard.

SEWARD: Mina, it's useless.

JONATHAN: Indeed, Mrs. Harker, don't stay. It is per-
ilous to be here when the moon creeps over the
grass and stands before me in all her nakedness.
Look at you! Thin already, like the tea after the
teapot has been watered.

SEWARD: Mrs. Harker it's time for you to go.

MINA: Good-bye, and I hope I may see you often, under auspices pleasanter to yourself.

JONATHAN: Good-bye, my dear. I pray God I may never
see your sweet face again. May he bless and keep
you.

She goes out and weeps.
Meanwhile back at the transfusion. SIMMONS
enters and sends QUINCEY *on his way.*

SIMMONS: The master's an odd duck, ain't he. Bet

he'd like to put his swizzle to you and he's not the only one neither. Workin' at this bloomin' place's makin' me loony myself, I reckon. Master Jack's a prig of the first water when 'e's not gassed out on the old chloral hydrate, and that's a fact. You want to play your *Ishtar* game in the garden tonight? Your lovely Wilhelmina is always makin' a nasty mess of the house and grounds with her continual regurgitation. And you know who's got to clean up all that filth. Reliable old Simmons here. Why, me mates at the Black Dog call me the rare sot for putting up with the lot of 'em: moon-calves, natures, bloody gooney-birds, I swear. Lookin' at you's got me pecker up, I do declare. I'm hot for a piece anytime, Miss Lucy. And that's the long and short of it. And that old cheese-monger from Hamsterdom leaves a regular splotch of piss every time he plants his fat arse. It's enough to make a bloke fly off his bloomin' nut.

JONATHAN *appears, pushing up the roof of his cell. He sings his song:*

There is hair growing into my head.
There is hair growing into my head
There is hair in the air;
It stands on a chair,
And then it grows into my head.

He slams the lid of his cell shut.
Intermission during which tea is served.

Act Two

Door Slam

 Late twilight on the East Cliff overlooking Whitby. LUCY *and* QUINCEY *sit at her favorite seat.*

LUCY: Oh, I do feel so thin I barely cast a shadow. Do you know poor Mina throws up everyday? Yes, she does. Every single day. It is quite revolting to be with her on these occasions. One must pretend not to notice. Her weak stomach must have something to do with the lamentable state of poor Jonathan. Quite changed they say he is. Do you suppose he is still capable of love? In the physical, gymnastical sense. Doesn't look it, to be sure. Looks quite the shorn sheep. But I have heard from Simmons, you know Simmons? Jack's man? That the mad are sexually indefatigable. Very goats at it. He described to me quite remarkable feats of copulation among the idiot population of his previous place of employment: Lady Gresham's Home for the Feeble-Minded. It was no point to stop the poor dears. They would, if prevented during sensible hours, get to it, clandestinely, at night. Till the very floors creaked.

The doctors tried straight-waistcoats, but the poor dears would roar and howl so it was more than decency could bear. And, goodness knows, what else would you have them do? The girls were quite clumsy and incapable of acquiring the simplest stitch—I am referring to needlecraft. The men absolute unlicked bears, lost to all possibility of Christian improvement. Simmons kept meticulous records of the more wonderful feats, the most appalling and exuberant lubricities. Simmons calls me *Ishtar* on our little walks over the wold. I make poor old Dr. Van Helsing do that too. He turns red as a beet, but he does it. Do you know he is quite incontinent? He must wear a sort of india-rubber night suit to avoid embarrassment. He calls it an attribute of a certain class of genius. Caesar. Alexander the Great. Willem the Silent. Bedwetters all. That's what dear Van Helsing has told me. I call him "Bobo." Then he pretends to do an examination of me—all because of my dreams, my apparent anemia, and the irritation about my throat.

Darkness. Wolf cries.

Lately, I have been restless at night, Quincey. Very restless. Good night.

Sings a phrase or two from her song.

I like when Simmons talks to me about the inmates at Lady Gresham's. Bonka, bonka, bonka, bonk.

Dracula 49

More wolf cries. DRACULA *alone in the sky.*

DRACULA: I am pure *otherness*. The ridiculous little sham of human conceit does not involve me. I am pure absence, and am immune to the petty anxieties which trouble the shallow waters of humanity. I hear the music of other worlds, and understand the deadly elegance of absolute nullity. He who opposes me becomes the fruit of my ceremonial banquet. I burn no bones before the altar of strange gods. I waste no blood in obscene and futile rites of propitiation. I am clean. I am honest. I do not suffer the inexact furies of the moving world. My dream is vast, empty, stationary, most cunningly articulated, infinitely mutable and transmutable. It was me and my kind, the high lords of Ckm Ckm, who have opened one inch the door of perpetuity, and slipped beyond, leaving behind on the doorstep of your civilization only the pathetic corpse of a dead rat. Nothing, absolutely nothing. For I am pure otherness.

Blackout. VAMPYRETTES *with flashlights light blood as it travels above the audience in clear pipes over to the transfusion machine.*

Another transfusion. Everyone rushes in. SIMMONS *reattaches* LUCY *to the machine as the blood flows. Blood everywhere.*

VAN HELSING: God! God! God! What have we done, what has this poor thing done, that we are so beset.

SEWARD: What does it all mean? I am beginning to wonder if my long habit of life among the insane is beginning to tell upon my own mind.

VAN HELSING: No. Today you must operate. I shall prepare. You are weakened already.

Takes off coat and rolls up sleeve.

QUINCEY: Jack Seward, I don't want to shove myself in anywhere where I've no right to be*; but I love that girl. What is it that's wrong with her? The Dutchman said, another transfusion of blood. That both you and he were exhausted. Is that not so?

SEWARD: Then please don't, you blithering idiot.

Pause.

That is so. What of it?

QUINCEY: I take it that both you and Van Helsing had already done what I did yesterday. Is that not so?

SEWARD: That's what we're trying to tell you, Quincey.

QUINCEY: I guess Miss Mina was in on it too. Four days ago she looked queer.

SEWARD: Oh shut up, Quincey, for God's sake.

QUINCEY: And how long has this been going on?

SEWARD: About ten days. What of it?

VAN HELSING: My friend John, be more calm. Our American Quincey, he have the child brain, but not malign.

MINA *staggers in, looking strange.*

Dracula 51

SEWARD: Oh, Quincey, you are an absolute...cowboy! If only you would pay attention you might keep abreast. It is the work of a vampire.

VAN HELSING: The wampyr "Dracula."

QUINCEY: What's a "wampyr"?

SEWARD: Vampire!

> *Music chord as* LUCY *lifts her little finger in a vampiric gesture.*
> VAMPYRETTES, *who have been watching, respond.*
> *Chord.*
> MINA *responds involuntarily.*
> *Chord.*
> LUCY *dies as all regard her with horror.*
>
> *Sound effect. Earthquake. Lighting flicker.*

VAN HELSING: Just as at the scholomance high in the air over lake Hermanstadt, the college of the undead. She is one of them now, God pity her.

> *Crossfade to the sky high above.* VAMPYRETTES *appear as* DRACULA *is on his way down to collect* LUCY. *They converse in draculan language.*

VAMPYRETTE 1: *Kckcptu ungld, vigboaou, o, Drkloa.*

DRACULA: *Tkctt, Bttl Krrk, Mcuaugan.*

VAMPYRETTE 2: *Qqqst?*

DRACULA: *Nx Krrrrcafxuoaoau. Nx grglc.*

> *Organ music comes in for dirge. The men take*

LUCY *off the machine and carry her in funeral procession. They sing.*

ALL: She's dead. We're sad. [*repeat*]

MINA: Just like poor Jonathan, sucked dry as a pressed hibiscus. A moment of silence for poor Jonathan.

Pause.

Dirge continues as all go out. DRACULA *takes* LUCY *from procession and leads her up to heaven and the* VAMPYRETTES.

Pause.

Insane surf music. DRACULA *and* LUCY *dance the twist.*

Blackout.

High on the East Cliff again. Gaslight. MINA *is unconciously twisting as Salvation Army music plays in distance.* SEWARD *watches in the twilight.*

SEWARD: Since our encounter, I have felt a strange new impulse, Mina. This monster, whatever he may be, has made me value my Christian soul the more. My days working with the twisted relics of lost reason have affected me, I fear. I must know if this thing truly exists. Van Helsing, I know, shall once more reap the recognition and rewards of our labors, if they do yield fruit. It is my lot; yet, perhaps, now, with the surety of your friendship, I can accept that lot. My father, you see, was a Hebrew, yes, a Hebrew of the Adelphi Theatre type. All that that phrase projects into one's brain: the Asiatic gown and fez, the greasy coin,

Dracula 53

the garbled injunction to buy cheap and sell dear; these instincts I have sought to transcend, through good Christian fellowship. Quincey and his crew, etc. But I cannot, I also confess, entirely escape my nature, even though it is other than I wish. Other than I do, in the bright days of my faith, deserve.

MINA: Oh, Jack.

SEWARD: So I shall, when this nasty business is done, take up the faith and seek out representatives of the Church of Latter Day Saints, so that God willing, I may journey to Africa once more and convert the dark man, and cleanse his wounds. And all within my brain will be "level with the horizon" as Van Helsing says. A feeling I have not known since the old days at Mbululand.

Pause.

I don't know, Mina. I really don't know.

MINA: It somehow eases me to write it all in words. To record it all, simply or not so simply, in figures of speech.

SEWARD: You're a pretty figure of a girl, Mina.

MINA: Was I very wanton?

Wolf cries.

Well, I suppose I should try to get some sleep. Good Night.

She waits for SEWARD.

Music.

She waits. DRACULA *appears.*

He seizes her and drags her to the center of the room, cuts his breast and forces her to drink like a kitten. She does.

DRACULA: Flesh of my flesh, blood of my blood. Drink.

Pause. She does. She likes it.

Good. When my brain says "come" to you, you shall cross land or sea to do my bidding.

MINA *drinks again.*

SIMMONS *and* SEWARD *return to* JONATHAN's *cell.*

SIMMONS: I think sir, his back is broken. See, both his right arm and the whole left side of his face are paralyzed.

SEWARD: Go and fetch Quincey, and send for Van Helsing.

SIMMONS: I can't understand two things. He could mark his face like that by beating his own head on the floor. I saw a young woman do it once at Lady Gresham's before anyone could lay hands upon her.

They winch door open to reveal JONATHAN *in a ghastly mess.*

Bloody waste that was as she was a rare piece. And I suppose he might have broke his neck by

Dracula   55

falling out of bed, if he got in an awkward kink.
But for the life of me! If his back was broke he
couldn't beat in his head; and if his face was like
that before his fall...

SEWARD: I think that will do for now, Simmons...

QUINCEY *enters.*

QUINCEY: My God, what happened to him?

VAN HELSING *enters.*

VAN HELSING: There is no time to lose. His words
may be worth many lives. It may be that a soul is
at stake.

SEWARD: I shall operate above the ear.

They winch him up to operate. He screams.

JONATHAN: I'll be quiet, Doctor. I have had a terrible
dream. And it has left me so weak that I cannot
move.

SEWARD: Go on.

VAN HELSING: Tell us your dream, Scardanelli.

JONATHAN: All day I waited to hear from him, but he
didn't send me anything, not even a blowfly. He
promised: "All these lives I will give to you and
many more if you will fall down and worship me."
But he came for her, for when she came to visit
me this afternoon she wasn't the same.

VAN HELSING: You are referring to Miss Lucy?

JONATHAN: No, I am talking about Mrs. Harker. She
reminded me of someone. A face from long ago.

Before I discovered fright in the dark interstices of the Borgo Pass. No, I must be mistaken. I know nothing of solicitors and their pretty wives. I like people with plenty of blood in them.

VAMPYRETTES *vowel chorus.*

So when he came tonight from Carfax I was ready for him. I have heard that madmen have unnatural strength; and as I knew I was a madman—at times anyhow—I resolved to use my power. He felt it too, for he had come out of the mist to struggle with me. He slipped through it, and when I tried to cling to him, he raised me up and flung me down.

SEWARD: We know the worst now. He is here in this house.

Door bang.

QUINCEY: Should we disturb her?

SEWARD: We must. If the door is locked we must break it in.

Door bang.

Mina, are you doing something in there that you don't want us to see?

MINA *appears, her face covered with blood.*

MINA: I was sleeping, Jack.

Dracula

SEWARD: In God's name, what does this mean?

JONATHAN: [*sings his swansong*] There is hair growing into my head, etc.

MINA: He's dead

VAN HELSING: God's will be done.

> *Chord.*
>   LUCY *suddenly appears, lifts her little finger.*
> MINA *responds involuntarily.* QUINCEY *faints dead away.*

LUCY: Come with me Jack. I want to kiss you and comfort you in my arms. Come we can rest together.

MINA: [*as in a trance*] He stepped out of the mist and said: "You may as well know it is not the first, nor the second time." And then he began to do it, and I felt my strength fade away.

SEWARD: Is this really Lucy's body or only a demon in her shape?

VAN HELSING: It is her body, and yet not it.

LUCY: Oh Jack, my love. I'm so glad to see you. I have seen things you never would believe. I have flown over London and Whitby. I can see through your eyelids into your brain; I can see what you are thinking. You are so unhappy in this place. Come with me. I have always loved you best. We are going to a wonderful new land in the West where there are no boundaries to one's will, and every type of energy is free to take on its own shape. Here you can only dry up, and be an inmate of your own brain. You must come with me.

VAN HELSING: Not for your life.

58   MAC WELLMAN

He holds up a wafer. She retreats in horror.

SEWARD: What is that you are using?

VAN HELSING: The Host. I brought it from Amsterdam.
I have an indulgence. Come, we must follow
quickly and catch them all before daybreak.

SEWARD: She is headed for the ruined chapel of
Carfax. Across the wold. Quincey, for God's sake,
wake up.

MINA: I took the opiate you gave me Jack, and was
dreaming of poor Jonathan, lost in the land beyond the forest.

> *Music.*
> *All rush out.*
> *Lighting change to Carfax Abbey.*
> *Music gets spooky.*
> VAN HELSING, SEWARD, QUINCEY and
> SIMMONS *appear with light bulbs.*
> *The* VAMPYRETTES *attack.* VAN HELSING
> *holds up the host. They retreat.*
> DRACULA *appears with suitcase and electric
> shaver.*

DRACULA: You think to baffle me, with your pale faces
all in a circle, like calves' heads in a butcher's
shop. You think you know who I am. But my name
is…TREMENDOUS. Ask your friend. Ah,
where is poor Jonathan?

> JONATHAN *appears hanging above his cell in a
> ghostly Cameo.*

Dracula   59

Would he have drunk the dark wine of eternity and joined us who simply ARE. The mad are other than you think, my proud level-headed pursuers.

There is no virus of the undead. Ckm. Ckm. You will never grasp anything of our ways. [*to* VAN HELSING] You silly leaking fraud. Your scholarship is as full of holes as the cheese of your native Gelderland. For you see I have observed you carefully from angles undreampt of in your physics, for I am nothing if not a student of life.

I must speak clear. I desire to go. Here now at this very moment. England, with it's sedgy pathways and stone fences, pleases me not. The blood is poor here, and I confess to a distaste for the bowler hat, which is such a passion in these parts.

VAN HELSING: [*advances with Host outsretched*] Monster, Wraith, whatever you are. Listen. We are weak men of 19th century, yes. Liars, yes. Lustful. It is true. Hypocrite. But we try to reach for the good. We are the collective voice of the light. You must back to the abysm from whence you sprang. My friends remember, if we fail, we become like him. Foul things of the night.

DRACULA: My colleagues and I desire a pledge of safe conduct.

> *He opens the adjacent coffin to reveal* LUCY.
> VAN HELSING *hastily returns to the men to consult.*

By the Bye. Your girls that you all love are mine

already but what a weak suffusion they are—a thin broth for so haughty an empire. This one, Miss Lucy Westenra... You may have her, but you must not interfere with our departure.

VAN HELSING *pockets the Host.*

The warlike days are over. Blood is too precious a thing in these days of dishonorable peace; and the stories of the great races are as a tale that is told.

He turns to go. QUINCEY *lunges at* DRACULA. *Who responds with one swift movement of his fingernail. Red sand spills out.* QUINCEY *collapses and slowly dies.*

Foolish, Mr. Morris. You are a peasant and so you must die like one.

Your land intrigues me, for there are fewer crucifixes there, and little garlic, with its noisome flower. If you must know, it is there I and my kin are journeying. America! Aboard the steamer *Paducah.* The crew is fat and flushed with blood. But you are a peasant. Die like one. I go now.

He goes. There is a huge shower of money. SEWARD *and* VAN HELSING *examine. Then in a strange coma* LUCY *starts to speak from within the coffin.*

LUCY: You must not forsake me. I have given up every-

Dracula 61

thing, my honor, my faith, my blood, my very life. All for you. They will snuff me out with no more compunction than boys kill cats. Drkloa, o, ccplp! Qmmnll! Oh, remember how much I adore you, my fire, my creator, my god, my sin. AM I TO SUFFER THE ABSOLUTE REJECTION OF MY LORD AND MASTER, FOR WHOSE SAKE MY SOUL SHALL BURN FOREVER IN THE FURNACE OF HELL!?

The men close in on her. They manhandle the coffin to a high place. VAN HELSING *prepares and takes out the hammer and stake.*

Mina! Mina! You mustn't let this happen. The blood is the joy, and I don't want my ridiculous Christian soul. Oh, Mina, I have flown, flown high above London and Whitby! Stop them! Mina! Mina! Oh, please stop them.

VAN HELSING: It will be a blessed hand that sets her free.

SEWARD: Tell me what I am to do.

VAN HELSING: Take the stake in your right hand. Place the point over the heart. Remember the cries of the mad are the secrets of God. Strike and send her to the stars.

Music.
SEWARD *drives the stake through her heart.*
They freeze as MINA *speaks.*

MINA: The body shook and quivered and twisted. The

sharp bright teeth clamped together until the lips were cut and smeared with crimson foam. But Jack never faltered, he looked like the figure of Thor as his untrembling arm rose and fell.

Music back in as SEWARD *resumes and screams return.*

It all wants order. Order and system, order and system and method. To fathom the doing Ckm Ckm. DRKLOA. XXXXXGHM.
Oh dear.
A moment of silence for poor Jonathan.

LUCY *is dead.*

Jack. I wonder if I may have the teeniest smidgin of chloral?
VAN HELSING: And now, my friend, brave lad, you may kiss her. Kiss her dead lips if you will. No longer is she the devil's undead. She is God's true dead, whose soul is with him.

SEWARD *bends to kiss* LUCY *he reappears covered with blood.*

He said the steamer *Paducah*, did he not? He's said to America, there to swell the grisly ranks of the undead. We must follow.

The men rush out roaring.
Pause.

Dracula 63

MINA: [*grinning broadly*] The room was dark. The bed was empty. She was only in her nightdress, but it seemed as though something dark stood behind the seat where the white figure shone and bent over it. For a moment I lost sight of her.

LUCY: [*appears from out of the coffin*] How strange it all was. My soul seemed to go out from my body and float about in the air. And I heard a lot of dogs barking, at once. I remember passing through the streets and over the bridge. A fish leapt as I passed by.

Lighting and sound effects for harbor as DRACULA *appears with suitcase.*

Ship's horn.

DRACULA *joins* VAMPYRETTES *on board ship who wave goodbye to us as jazz band plays "And When the Saints."*

END OF PLAY

Swoop

Swoop premiered at the SoHo Repertory Theatre in New York, November 1994, with the following cast:

DRACULA	John Nesci
WILHEMINA MURRAY (as her higher nature)	Zivia Flomenhaft
WILHEMINA MURRAY (as her id)	Jan Leslie Harding
LUCY WESTENRA	Lauren Hamilton

Directed by Julian Webber. Sets and Lighting: Kyle Chepulis. Costumes: James Sauli. Sound: John Kilgore. Original Music: David van Tieghem. Assistant Director: Tim Farrell. Production Stage Manager: Christine Lemme.

To bite into the world with no other "care" than the habit of biting, isn't that entering the world? What a grasp of the world is a bite.

The ancient cosmologies do not give order to thoughts; they are audacious reveries, and in order to bring them back to life it is necessary to learn to dream again.

BACHELARD, *Reverie*

*

God contains bad stuff.

M. YANDELL SMITH, *Dicta*

Persons of the play:

DRACULA, A WAMPYR, under various pseudonyms,
    and his companions:
WILHEMINA MURRAY, as her Higher Nature and a
SECOND MINA, as her Id—in disarray—and
LUCY WESTENRA, also undead and happy.

*

The action of *Swoop* (such as it is: flapping mainly)
takes place on a cool and windless night some seven
miles up, above the island of Manhattan.

The time is the present, whatever that is.

Scene one. In the darkness we hear a vampiric voice:

I picked up the band of totality—blessed darkness!—in the Gulf of Mexico and proceeded North into the wilds of Texas after it. The band stretched some 211 miles wide and prolonged itself North-North-East at some 350 yards per second, with me for a companion…. Within a few hours I would be directly overhead the fabulous cities of Northeastern America….

Lights up slowly. We see a long, dark MAN'S *white face in the sky. Below him is the dimly lit surface of what appears to be a dinner table, covered with a white table-cloth. (Actually, we are seven miles up in the air, and the table is the island of Manhattan.) He smiles and makes a welcoming gesture with one hand, also very white. Pause.*

DRACULA: My name is Moral Shadow Witherspoon and my family is an old one, older I sometimes think than even the figure of Adam. That clinched nail in the mind of our Creator, the defiler of polyphonous pagany, that eremite gasbag—Jehovah the Monotheist. I shall not trouble you with my own personal story. Aside from which, it has

slipped my mind. Can't recall it. I am an aristocrat. Being an aristocrat carries with it a certain
hat. And certain other hats. Then there is the
improvement of the, um, species, which had better be left to those still bamboozled by the empty
promise of the future, television, and the mark-
ing down of domestic comestibles, fur and all
such like; those capable of...empathic fraud. To
enter into the mind of another is crime, an act of
breakage and entropy. So, there you have it, in a
nutshell, the very pith of my philosophy, free of
all cant.

Pause.

For, in truth, aren't we all complicit in this
phantomnation? You, and you, and you. All ani-
mated by the ferocious need to make impact on
the surface of a strange planet that hovers beneath us like a blur. It is, indeed, a world of blur
that hovers beneath our dancing feet. For once I
journeyed among the wise, and spoke of Hegel,
Harry Martin, the Master of the Yellow Parasol,
and Maurice the Geek of Nones, who crept into
the unlatched mail-box of the Protophotophagoi.
All this is as clear to me as Rome was to Remus,
as Tarsus to Paul.

Pause.

Why, you ask, why do you hold us, a sea of the
unseeing, here, in thrall? Why, indeed. There is

Swoop 71

an old saying that runs roughly thus…I do not recall the saying, nor is it a particularly memorable one, but it very much cuts to the quick, it marks the spot, it blackens the spilled blood with the soot of apparence: "Your dog is in the sky. So is mine." That dog forewarns us of the necessary idea, the concrete bailiwick of the emboldened, who are maddened by reference to things, special things. Great stupid, unarguable facts.

Pause.

I was not always thus, a zoophagous maniac. In the old days, in my lord's fastness of Ckm Ckm, I and my kind would feast upon the standard fare. Mamaliga. Potage of leeks and potatoes. Often a roast chicken done up curiously with paprika. The virulent paprikas of the Magyars.

Pause.

The taste for blood became fashionable only in the last century. At the apex of our true celebrity. In truth, I was never very fond of the stuff, and it is no small trick, even with pointy teeth, to pierce the skin and vein of a terrified, thrashing, human being and not make quite a mess of things in the doing. "Blood is the life," indeed! One might just as well proclaim: "A bucket of soapy water, a bloody towel and a mop are the life." Definitely a disagreeable and totally unsanitary operation, totally out of character for one such as myself. An aristocrat. An aesthete. A classicist and lover of the tidy, even if viewed from an extreme Dionysian,—not to say—demonic, perspective.

Pause.

And while we are on the subject of "taste," permit me a small culinary digression. Not all bloods taste the same. Not to speak of nutritive value. Unless one is built, gastroenterologically speaking, along the lines of a leech, one is not likely to derive much in the way of sensual delectation from such a diet. It is true some bloods have a certain sweetness, a certain delicate aroma and savor, but these are rare. Young children and those fortunate enough to have enjoyed tranquil milk-and-honey, cornfed lives in sunny climes filled with laughter and azaleas. These are rare, and their blood is rare. Can you imagine the hideous reek of a sixty-year-old, gouty Englishman, grown fat on Scotch egg, broiled goose, and Yorkshire pudding? Not to mention the unspeakable curries and grey, soggy vegetables of that realm. Port wine, the stench of cigars and indecipherable sweetmeats. Such blood ought to be thrown out with the contents of the chamber pot. Such blood contains about as much of the *elan vital* as the fluid which is drained out of automobiles during the ritual oil change. Extreme old age may be a factor in my distaste, but I was never really fond of the stuff. I was too much a conformist in

Swoop 73

my youth. A slave to fashion. Clearly there is much in my life I would like to forget. The sleeplessness of the vampire is a classic instance of the poetic entelechy of bad conscience.

Pause.

Actually, My true name is Aloysius Nancarrow Flowerpot, and I do not drink blood at all, but subsist on unsweetened lemonade and mashed potatoes. Cold mashed potatoes. Cold, wet, soggy, mashed potatoes. And these only to maintain bulk, and fluid level. Real undead nutrition is acquired by frequent doses of an invisible ether discovered originally in our ancient homeland of Kush, but re-discovered since on every continent but one, Antarctica. This invisible ether is available commercially under the trademark name of "Swank." Informally, we always refer to it as "geezer" gas, since the stuff is an effluent by-product of the ageing human mind, considered as an obsessive, hypertrophic thought-machine, caught up in the endless loop of remorse, recrimination, and the nameless archaic dread that is incurred upon contemplation of happiness among the young, and otherwise unafflicted. "Geezer" gas allows us to bridge the gap between appearance and apparence. Between hard fate, and a more romantic destiny. In a word, the inhalation of "geezer" gas allows us to have our cake and bite it, too. If the living knew our secret they would elect us to public office and worship us like the rich. For we are much alike, and we pass among them, undetected. Much as they pass among us, undetected.

Pause.

For a long time I have been an ardent traveller. I arrived in this country after a long voyage on the steamer, *Paducah,* out of Charleston. I played the part of an eccentric European gentleman with a fondness for cryptic parables, off-color jokes, and an unusual and deep knowledge of lunar eclipses, often dating back to remote centuries before the Christian epoch. My ability to recall amazingly precise details from, say, a pleasant October evening, near twilight, say, on a seaside villa on the Golden Horn in the Year of Our Lord 802 caused, first, skepticism, then a certain pall of uncanniness among the crew and my acquaintances among the passenger list. I would lay, wrapped in a tartan quilt, curled up in apparent ease, on the sundeck, occasionally playing checkers with Williams, chess with Wu, or faro with Father Wallace of the Roman Catholic Church. And this despite the strength I possessed to lift the ship out of the sea, and fling the entire hulk from horizon to horizon without raising so much as a bead of sweat upon my strange, withered brow. I thought a long time about friends from shadowy times, dead languages, the odds against discovering the meaning of love, worn sandals, broken headstones, cast-off items of

Swoop 75

clothing such as singleton socks, and the slow ectotopy of old hats, hats from the era of Bismarck and Castlereagh, hats from the day of Talleyrand and Thermidor. Hats from Constantinople. Hats from the days of the Paleologi. Hats from Paphlagonia. Hittite and Assyrian hats. Clasps. Thorns. Buckles. Thread. Tacks. Needles. Blades. Boxes of black pearls and broken teeth. Delicate bones of small animals.

Pause.

My real name is Royal Treatment Doodad, and although I and my kind are, yes, derived from the ancient nobility of Kush, by way of the Carpathians, in truth, we appeared on this continent, suddenly, by means of time's Worm-Hole, which deposited us, I mean we—in the sense of "I"—suddenly one day in the summer of 1936 on a dusty sidewalk in Sioux City, Iowa. I found myself sprawled out, in the garb of a Fuller Brush Man. A battered wicker suitcase containing samples lay beside me in the dustbowl dirt. A straw hat, presumably mine also, spun like a child's top on the diametric axis of its brim. Three years later I was a pillar of the community, owned forty-thousand acres of the finest grazing land, the finest house on the finest street, was the nominee of the Republican Party for Governor, was betrothed to the prettiest girl in town, the Mayor's daughter, and kept my coin stacked neatly in a little, walnut chest, inscribed in mystic runes from ancient Kush. No one had guessed my secret. I was safe. A hidden geyser of "geezer" gas in the nearby Callithumpian Mountains sated my unholy hunger. No one noticed my craving for cold mashed potatoes and unsweetened lemonade. Indeed, these peculiarities of my diet were deemed virtuous instances of sober moderation in the wilderness of the monster beefsteak and the howling conboberation attendant upon enormous consumption of rye whiskey. My bitey nature, however, could not contain itself. Tooth must do the work of tooth. It is nature, working through us, even though we fall up or down, through time's Worm-Hole, in myriad disguises of identity. Even if, when we go in search of ourselves, like olden Heraclitus, we find nothing there but an ancient tomcat transmogrified to a pincushion.

Pause.

So, as the man of the world, Royal Treatment Doodad, I prospered mostly. I bit, but little. Bit only when I must, and only to hurt and harm, never to draw blood, particularly not Siouxian City blood, which was very poor and ratchety, being curdled by too much bleach, bible reading, and square dancing. I do, however, admit I bit upon the neck, hard, of my fiancee, Penelope Angelsfood Birdswater, daughter of Clyde Birdswater, the Mayor of Sioux City; for which act I was unceremoniously tarred and feathered,

Swoop 77

and run out of town on a rail; yes, although these things are true, they are only trivially true, and not adamantly true. As they ought to be. The lack of that adamant is my mitigating modality.

Pause.

Further, the precise circumstance of that mitigating circumstance was the obvious truism that before I took up the habit of biting, and began to bite, I too was bitten, savagely bitten and chewed about the throat.

A purely innocent pause.

So: I am an innocent. The last in a series of thought-objects percolated untimely from the cosmic mire. I am merely engaged in perfecting my nature, which is to bite, digress, imbibe "geezer" gas, eat cold mashed potatoes, drink the most insipid of lemonades and flap about, high in the foetid skies of the tri-state area, New York and New Jersey mainly, looking for a creature, far below, to bite.

Pause.

Among my favorite pastimes is the systematic scrutiny and collation of certain of the more remarkable instances of partial or complete obscuring, with relation to a designated draculan observer, of one celestial body by another. I collect eclipses. Among my most favorite eclipses are the following: the Ghost lunar of Felix. AD 303 or 4. About the time of the martyrdom of St. Felix. The Happy.

Pause.

My other favorites: A fine, lunar eclipse in the year 969 in Iraq. Tabit, son of Sinan, saw it and said the moon was totally eclipsed on the night of Thursday, the 14th of Rajab, at Babylon. Tabit is mistaken: the eclipse occurred on Friday, at around midnight. Several centuries later, I picked up a marvelous annular eclipse in the Pacific Ocean just north of Easter Island. Flapping madly only a few hundred yards above the wine-dark sea I followed to a point half-way across New Mexico, where both eclipse and me—the image of myself, that is—were recorded by an Anasazi craftsman in a set of petroglyphs. This was on the fifth of April, 1102˚AD. The boulder bearing these petroglyphs has unfortunately been lost. It lies buried under a heap of worthless rubble near the old Three Rivers service station at US 54 north of Tularosa.

Pause.

More recent eclipses have been, by and large, disappointing, mere echoes of a grander music that is past, and shall be no more.

Swoop 79

He slowly fades from view as the lights come up on WILHEMINA MURRAY, *the first of her two vampiric selves. She now leads the flight.*

FIRST MINA: I know what you are thinking. You are thinking she is dead. Dead and yet not so. How pitiable. How sad. To be plucked from her respectable life, and her respectable engagement with that fine young solicitor, Jonathan Harker, and her fine, solid, respectable, predictable nineteenth century. Plucked like an unripe fig, before her time. I confess I would not undo my dark turn from the merely human for a wilderness of monkeys. Think on that: for a wilderness of monkeys.

She laughs oddly.

True, the good Count has gone gaga, true. True, the impulse to feed has ruled out some of the refinements thought essential to more or less civilized behavior. True, I have become, more or less, a monster of appetite, strapped to the wheel of my hot, carnal need. But even before my turn, is it not a fact that this is how the fine, noble, Nineteenth Century regarded me? Become what you seem, the saying goes. I have become what I seemed, seemed to those who saw in my innocence only spite, only appetite. But now I do the biting. For I must.

Pause.

Sometimes I feel as though I had been swimming in time, as though it were a clear fluid. A palpable substance, both hindering and supporting one's motor control. Decades like waves in the ocean, beating upon a shore that is the Inconceivable. The rush of meaningless events, wars, atrocities, the useless obsession with dates, facts, and slightly prurient information concerning one's neighbors. The hideous redundancy of fashion, with its vapid and supercilious alternation of hats, ideas, shoes, and highflown rhetoric. Its shabby conceits. The sanctimonious pursuit of what is called "truth" by the parsimonious inheritors of wealth, power, privilege or other idiotic additive tropisms. Lust for the finite. The endless mediocre puppet show of apparent choice versus apparent error. The cruel slaughter of innocence in the name of stupidity, and even innocence.... A thing of no worth...like a flashlight buried in muck, at the bottom of the sea.

Pause.

For in truth we do inhabit a world of blur, a world of vague, insubstantial entities, and this is apparent once one has had the nerve to harden oneself a bit, and examine what passes for reality with a little critical...with a little skepticism. All the hubbub of the Moving World amounts to mere perturbation, a slightly exasperating surface tension vertically rendered on the horizontal face of a small, insignificant pond that is quietly freezing over.

Swoop   81

Pause.

Wilhelmina. Mina. Strange, I do not seem able to recall my own last name. My patronymic. The name of my father. Who was my father, for in truth I possess none, now that I am *vlkoslak,* undead, one of the High Ladies of Ckm Ckm. A world adrift inhabited by evil cats and evil cockatoos the color of pure ionization. Butterflies with razor wings. Gigantic palaces of time-mottled chert and schist, draculan towers of adamant, floating above the streaming rubble of the red wind. Magyar music rattling up from cisterns of Empty Time out of antique celestas and barrel organs. *Vlkoslak,* vampire. A world like a child's spinning top, spinning so rapidly as to appear quite motionless. A world beyond the palaver of easy comprehension.

Pause.

All my life I worked diligently, within the moral framework of the time, to record and systematize experience, perceptual data as I was familiar with it, all with some mad dream of a secular paradise shortly to come. All of us, in that lacquered world of Victorian omnisciencia, saw in ourselves the culmination of thirty centuries' blind struggle for total mastery, accomplishment, and the achievement of a unifying theoretical framework. I suppose this was a noble refraction. I suppose it gave my life purpose, along with the law which provided sense and realism to my fiance's life. Poor, sad Jonathan, he is a shadow now, an echo of an echo, moving like a crow's shadow among wisps and merds of a wasteland in the old world of blur.

Pause.

I do think, sometimes, on how hard I have become, how resistant and resilient a thing the soul is once one has deleted the "human" component. But the feeling is of an enormous transcendental lift. As though one had suddenly acquired truly human dimension after centuries of dull, insipid sub-human existence in the carapace of a bug or beetle. For it is a thing gone truly mad that spins our child's top, and stops only to hear the wind creep in the wheat, wriggle on the apple bough, and sizzle in the reeds, as it inscribes its riddle on the blank stone rock faces of the Hebrides, in the cold clutch of the horrid seas, for none to unravel and read.

Pause.

An enormous transcendental lift, yes. Still I confess I do miss the odd flow and convection of hot winds you call "politics" even though I am not partial to what are termed "contracts," "litigation," "settlements," "negotiation" and the like, or other forms of compromise. Prattle pays in the world of blur, I observe. But in the Stationary World we have no need for this. And not for a wilderness of monkeys would I change places with

Swoop   83

the most high among you. You, and you, and you.
You, my former friends and playmates. You, my
former confidants, friends, countrymen. The stuff
of my affable, companionable food.

Pause.

An enormous transcendental lift, yes. The nature of that lift we call the "draculan," and the
change it causes in Simple Time—Simple Human Time—simpleton mediocre time is, frankly,
tremendous. Our time is Time Turned, Draculan
Time. A dradical redaction of time's tune to our
vampiric exigency. These ripples signify the snake
of time's force, the Snake Time wriggling and
worming its way through the obdurate oppression of perceived reality. At least as it comes to
be exemplified in your world. The world of food.
We of the Stationary World consist in an order
you could not fathom. This, I suspect, is why
names peel off of us, like old cellophane, like unnecessary labels, and flutter off. To be a "Mina"
means no more or less to me than "anima." My
personal nomenclature redacts a fritillary of the
far away. An anima of otherworldliness arrayed
in a fair figure, as you behold, above you to image the draculan.

Pause.

If you would bounce a child's ball in our world,
that ball would go on bouncing forever unless

stopped by some intervening force. But to deduce from this peculiarity of our draculan physics some implication of a merely mortal consistency would be foolish. Our fine, dear Count here, who styles himself "Deville" to wow the ladies in Picadilly Circus, this bloodless avatar of the draculan, has given it to be known that he subsists on cold mashed potatoes and an odd etheric substance known as "geezer" gas. Ha! But nothing causes me such gastronomical thrill as the eating of plump, white housecats. You would be amazed how many unappetizing objects resemble the plump, white housecat when viewed from a vertical elevation of, say, seven miles, on a cool and windy, moonlit night. When one is hungry, the urge to metaphysical speculation must be put aside, for a time, so that we satisfy the most low of our creaturely cravings.

Pause.

But there is nothing like a brace of plump, white housecats, freshly killed along with a magnum of the finest champagne. Nothing. Nothing can measure up to it. This vile drug called "Swank" is only used by those addicted to a conception of the past as conditioned totally by inane tribal confabulations. But massive doses of the stuff simply appall the mind, not to mention one's aesthetic center of gravity. Moderation in all things rules the day, even in the realm of the draculan, ruled by the law of wriggle.

Swoop

Pause.

When I was a little girl, and had not yet been bitten, I suppose I might have felt...no...I suppose things might have turned out differently. I suppose the person I was then, if she had known, might have had a terror of whom she was to become,—at whom of who—of who I am now. I know I possessed seven very frilly, white crinoline dresses, absolute horrors of the creaking fashion of the time—which I quite enjoyed. And a little brass rabbit, a creature modelled on some idiotic children's book, which I would play with, and cause to hop about, thus.

She demonstrates.

To hop about, thus. Hop about thus and so to my unstinting amusement. Can you imagine! A thing of brass modelled into the shape of a mere rabbit. A toy some two or three inches in height, which I would cause to hop about on the window sill, of a green and gold summer's day. How far away have my elongations taken me, how far, far, far. Hop and hop and....

Pause.

But this vast, indescribable metropolis, always brings me back to now. This non-rabbity New York. Non-rabbity now, where I must burrow and tunnel my way through the most loathsome filth and offal to have any chance of securing even one unplump and mangy housecat. Yes. This New York. This non-rabbity New York. For while I love to soar and glide for long periods of time at a great height above the metropolis, as I am now, in truth most of my time is spent burrowing and tunnelling beneath the asphalt crust, in the dark primordial interstices of her nether world, as a sort of fabulous draculan mole. My chronic chthonic excavations have taken me deep into the city's forgetfulness. I have come to know the true secret history of your olden times. Slit throats, gunshot wounds, random hackings and blunt stabs, the bodied consequence of long, unimpeded descents down elevator shafts and factory staircases. Arson, barbarous suppression of strikes and riots, oppression and wicked crimes against orphans, widows, Africans and the North American red man. I find odd bits of evidence that chronicle both the howls and demented fury of the luckless, and the disingenuous boast of the saved. Broken eyeglasses of twisty wire, bent scissors, scraps of leather and fur, shreds of old newsprint from a burnt mattress, a rimless black hat, a brass clasp, tweezers, shoelaces from a time now lost. A broken clay pipe squenched with a plug of char.

Suddenly an awkward pause.

Astarte. Azrael. Avant garde. I think I shall slide behind the moon for a time in order to become

Swoop

another person. A person more to your liking. Perhaps you will indulge me in this phantom whim, the significance of which I shall enlarge upon when I reappear. Shortly. I shall return presently. Entertain yourselves as you will. The moon is bright, and the night is fair...I promise to return with a delicious surprise...Astarte. Azrael. Avant garde.

Pause. Cheesy "wampyr" music. House lights on. All stage effects cease as she walks offstage, or behind a screen. After a brief time she reappears, the SECOND MINA *that is (her draculan inner self). She has a applied ghastly make-up. Snaps her fingers, and we return to the skies above New York.*

SECOND MINA: I have returned, and am different. I am the same, but different.

Pause.

Although the truth is, I was not the one who bit: I was bitten. Not that I have any problem with who I am. Nope, not me. And my teeth hurt. Biting is hard on teeth, and I'm no spring chicken, I know. Maybe I'll have to stop eating housecats. Maybe eating housecats has ruined my teeth. Would you get a load of my teeth. Big Choppers. I used to have these dainty, white, pearly teeth. The kind moonstruck poets used to write about. But after my "turn," that's a miserable euphemism for being bitten—after my turn my teeth got big and nasty. Maybe I'll have to give up eating plump, white housecats. Really is a disgusting habit, if you think about it. Maybe I'll just give up eating tomcats. Tomcats really are rancid. They disgust even me. I'm not without compunctions. Only, it's hard to tell them apart from seven miles up on a cold and partly-cloudy moonlit night. You can just barely make them out because the earth gives off a faint, preternatural glow. As though it were alive. Giordano Bruno thought the world was alive. They burnt him at the stake in February 1600 in Rome. I was there, in the *Campo di Fiori,* in 1600. The "Field of Flowers" in English. It was a fairly cold day. A day like one of Giotto's frescoes. The reality of it bursting from newly wrought lines of mathematical perspective. I thought I saw the Pope, Clement VIII, but it probably wasn't him. Anyhow, I watched Bruno sizzle. I was glad they roasted him. The heretic. He knew too much. People who know too much all ought to burn. He said the earth moves because it is alive. That's enough for me. Burn the heretic. Freedom of speech for those who can afford it, and those who watch what they say. I know what I'm talking about, since being who I am, with these big monster teeth, I nose about in places most people don't even know exist, and therefore have no conception of. Reality's not holding up so well. Cause and effect are coming apart. Time's Worm has a bad case of being hypnotized, like the chicken, by the long white stripe in the middle of the road.

Swoop

Pause.

Still, there is tradition. Obligation. Duty. All those time-worn cliches. Charity. Blah-blah. Social imagination. Social conscience. Sensitivity.

She laughs drily.

Think about sensitivity when you've got a full set of ivory gondolas in your mouth. A smile that will not refrain. Because none of the High Lords and Ladies of Ckm Ckm had any clue as to the true, pathetic essence of time's tangle of twine. Nor the unrelenting terror of its rope-a-dope. Nor the incredible paucity of places of escape: emerald isles looted by our fiducial superiors, gleaming desert panoplies swarmed upon by larval spiritual shipwrecks, devotees of crystal pyramid. Abject transcendental has-beens. Even the majestic polymodality of the skies now retains only a backlit semblance of its former significance, a waking nightmare for air-traffic controllers....All of it, gone rabbity. Rancid. The wheels and levers of falsehood all too in evidence just beyond the meadow of green velours, and the crude mechanical show of the cloud and wind machines, flapping, flapping, flap....

Pause.

Time passes, and there are certain things which I reflect upon, and which thus considered give me a certain pleasure. My favorite book of medicine is the *Kiranides,* from the twelfth century, which contains a recipe for a LICINIUM or combustible compound in whose light those present will appear to one another like flaming demons. Or, in book two, where the reader is instructed that wearing the dried tongue of a weasel inside his socks will close the mouths of his enemies. The last, smallest, and most elegant of my favorite things is to lead the Little-Leaf Beetle—slowly—all the way, all the way to Hell.

Pause. Her Higher Nature returns.

I have returned, and am different.
I am the same, but different

The two VAMPIRES *sing a little Song*:

> The devil has beautiful skin.
> She ties her face in a bow.
> She knots the bow to her knees.
> Then she tears up the picture
>   and paints her face again.
> The devil has beautiful skin.

> The devil has beautiful skin.
> First she grows fat,
> Then she grows thin.
> Then she tears up the picture
>   and paints her face again.
> The devil has beautiful skin.

Swoop 91

> Your dog is in the sky. So is mine.
> What a great first line. Too bad
> there are no others.

Both fade as lights come up on the third vampire, LUCY WESTENRA.

LUCY: Chew this over. In the beginning there was the act of biting. I am called "Lucy Westenra" but in truth I am child only of the act of biting, and to this act, and its delectable repetition, I bow and pay homage; I do think I am the happiest girl who ever trod the surface of the Moving World, or put tooth to vein, or flew high above, in the mute, star-flecked diaphane. What masticates incarnadines. What chews transcends the blues and unbottles the Djinn of oral delights. So, when I overhear my dreary brethren, high above Central Park as we sail high and low in vast bloody loops, where no one has the wit to spy, I cannot resist a cry for sheer hilarity.

She cries out.

People are so afraid of death. But believe me, there is nothing they are more afraid of than a young girl, who is very pretty, very wanton, and knows what exactly she wants. Particularly, when she is dead. Certainly I have no recollection of being bitten by the good Count "Deville." We sat on the stone chair high on the East cliff overlooking the whole harbor of Whitby, and he talked of some strange gas, and of the "guisers," strange old men and children, who would inhale the stuff, and put on strange, corny masks and perform in bad plays. He smelled of sauerkraut and paprika, and seemed ill. Mina, who was a friend, at the time, suggested he was a celebrated personage from an obscure region in Central Europe, the Carpathian mountains, I believe, rich as Croesus, and that therefore I should be receptive. Rubbish, I thought. Why is it a girl undergoes such a peculiar transformation from the decided hellion that, at age ten, can beat up any boy on the block, play football, and do large sums in her head to boot: fearless, reckless, outspoken, cheerful and quick to action; when by sixteen she is smothered in clichés of domesticity, ribbons and bows, afraid of spiders? Cautious. Simpering. A thing dependent on the whims of others, and happy most when cowering in shadows.

Pause.

So: the gothic traditions of the vampiric have no appeal to me. I happen from moment to moment and have no use for fixed conceptions of myself. But then I don't place much reliance on what people say or do. What they do is usually a perfect horror in pure performance terms, and that holds true whatever culture we are discussing. It all boils down to the same, sad song-and-dance. Masks and realism, sincerity, lectures. This is the way to do this, that is the way to do that.

Swoop   93

Habits posing as precepts. Repetition upon repetition of the too, too familiar as some kind of
brake upon what might overwhelm. Since I find
frailty and fragility the stuff of timeless clichés, I
have little patience for what passes for innocence.
Occasionally I move with great, shocking celer-
ity, if only to cause a refreshing response. Animals and sea creatures behave pretty much like
human beings, but are somehow better at it because perhaps they don't always try too hard. Birds
used to amuse me because they too fly, and their
thoughts are usually more elegant, or at least
more concise, than those of bipeds, or quadru-
peds like cats and dogs, and other Americans.

Pause.

Since I am prolonged through the medium of
time in unexampled ways, I suppose I should be
able to say something on the topic of intelligent
life. Other intelligent life. In the hidden sector.
Down there we behold a city. Full of noses, gaudy
stuff, people of all hues, characters attached to
the sad filth of their lives, money, cheeses, rats, a
few wolves, unspeakable neckties, unreadable
books on this and that. All of them relate to a
central organism they call the state—by a long
sad, spiritual membrane. A resting place of their
odd faith. To grasp, emphatically, at a sunset as
though it were a utensil. To measure one's reach
by lacks; what one desires, but lacks. As though
the moon were a footstool to kneel upon in self-

regard, while the thing of wonderment roars, and roars, and wings it outside. Don't chew on this for all I care. What is stabbed by tusk knows fate's no nicety of wriggle. Those that loved me died unloved because I choose not to release one small radical root from a hypothetical quadratic. The business about castles of chert and schist is not true, nor do we dive down and hook fine, white housecats. Or, at most rarely. We fancy—in the main—plumpy DRAMATURGOS. Yet to pin down the draculan disremembers its furry edge, and grows a hatful of spikes, thorns, and scotch tape branched into colorless, translucent roses. Who cares if the nightmare you dreamt up to torment your enemies is only a fluid poured down a drain? Who cares if no one loves you anymore? What did THEY ever know, the beloveds? Did the two of you ever speak the same moral language? Did they ever obey you when you made the universal sign of indication over their round, expectant faces? Did they ever memorize the deep truths you told them when they were heartsick, and took to bed, fearing the worst, with the multitude of their dollars stacked up for the doctors and law-yers who steal hope in the name of the republic? Who are they? Who are you? What difference does any of it make if you choose to oppose iron by teeth and forge your own law, a thing of can-openers, thistles, missed opportunities, shoelaces and the side-show acts thought up by the late Dauphin of France to simultaneously retrace and erase his tracks. Why, if all that I recall of my

Swoop 95

people makes me loathe both them and me, why, why should I not dare to aspire to the frauds who use their shapes in the obscene parodies? And don't the parodies themselves suggest something we would just as soon forget about transcendence itself? And we knew the full horror. And we did not know. And we were moved, and we felt nothing. And we heard the music and thought it din. And we were deaf. And we were glad we were deaf. The monster who disguises your daughter like one you would spear with golf clubs has his eye on your car. The one who doubts the riddle of turbulence will find her house riven by molecular derision. The one who stumped your daddy on your granddaddy's knee is watching from the mailbox where she's been hiding for years, and she has the same question for you she had for all the others and you know you don't know. And you know if you admit the fact your goose is cooked. Your goose is truly cooked because you haven't a clue whose bed you've been sleeping in, nor with whom, nor whose insane laughter accompanies whose strange coughing, fits and delirium, out of doors, on the street, this very night, twenty years after Fate passed you by.

Pause.

But I am getting ahead of myself. This high up you hear nothing from below; that is the point I was making with my draculan digression. The optick on the city is transposed, forensically, under the rubric of the edible. Below, spread out in rapturous, jazz-age neon and the glitter of a martini silverado, lies the city of New York. Fabulous. High flyers like ourselves. High rollers in the gaming clubs. Bottom dwellers in the news rooms and faculty dining houses. The abject pruners of the flock, leaning against street lamps, at remote corners, their Uzis and MAC 10s on safety. Bankers and profiteers spewing forth the electronic, hieroglyphic papyrus of princely camouflage, all sharing in a sense the same hyperpsychodermic needle. Manufacturers and purveyors of thought-objects strutting their wares. It is a need to prey that so incessantly needles...needles some to madness, awful woes and bellowing, and some other, happy few, notably me, to my sustaining updraft, my hilarity. I look down through veil upon veil of wispy vapor and behold a city of food.

Pause.

The glowing metropolis. Isn't it beautiful? Isn't it truly fabulous? Indeed, the entire tri-state area makes my mouth water, which is the prime mover for my gladness. We are reputed to stem, in tribal terms, from the last of the fallen angels. But the true crime of Those Who Fell was not rebellion, but joyousness and bright waggery. The other side, our foes, believed in order, starch, and the grimmest of grim decorum. Obedience. Little stars on the forehead for proper conduct, meekness, and the hackneyed sanctimony of the downward-focussed gaze.

Swoop

Pause.

For the devil, you may recall, was a little fellow, a child of brightness, hilarity, and pure investigation. This led him to certain oral pleasures deemed unseemly by the management. Hence his—and our—sudden removal from the attic of heaven. Our version has it that we left of our own accord, and they (above) would have us back in a minute. Our direct ancestor was the last to fall, according to heavenly legend. Our oldest saying says: "One fell...and swoop!" Never touched the ground—that is, the floor of the fiery pit, hell itself—but flew far away, over the forests, lakes, and abysses of the known world, past the glittering facade of the ice mountains to a place in central Asia, ancient Kush.

Pause.

Ah, but to look down the long line that extends from the tip of one's draculan nose, down the elegant vector of immaculate rectilinearity, down to the city of one's food, city of one's delight, the site of one's perennial theater of mandibular excitation; that is happiness—that is happiness exponentially enlarged.

Pause.

Happiness is the truest artifice. Happiness is doubt in the face of the supposed. Happiness is the refusal to take seriously what one ought.

Happiness is a squirt of squid's ink in the baptismal fount of the shit-named. Happiness is a pocketful of marbles, a rain of belly-buttons in the empty stadium of the team that moved away. Happiness is the arc of error, repeated till it rings true. Happiness is the coffin lid, closed for all time.

Pause.

All the letters of the alphabet are footprints of demons who arrived here millennia ago disguised as lemons, arrayed in spectral starlight. Seeing themselves, naked, they dispersed. Some of them are hidden among you, happy. One of them fell. Rose to high rank. I am she. I glow. O is O and nothing more. Demons inhabit the intersection of circles, as we do. We recognize each other, in the unholy starburst of our secret LICINIUM, even in the towering chill, seven miles above the dreaming metropolis, by our incurable happiness and our inclination to bite, bite.

Pause.
Reprise of the Song.

The devil has beautiful skin, etc.

DRACULA: Enough. Enough of this chatter. Look below. Can you spy what I spy? Geezer gas.

Hands binoculars to MINA. *She looks, roars. She hands binoculars to* LUCY, *who also roars.*

Swoop 99

MINA: See, below, the lumpy and unwary DRAMA-
TURGO,* loitering like a fine…white housecat….
SECOND MINA: Like a fine, white housecat. By the
stagedoor of the Public theater.

She roars.

DRACULA: Geezer Gas.

He swoops.

LUCY: Let us swoop down and descend in a fit of per-
pendicular prolongation. Let us descend in a fit
of pure bliss.

*All swoop and are gone. We hear a scream from
far below. Slow black.*

END OF PLAY

MAC WELLMAN

Described by the *New York Times* as "a playwright intoxicated with words," Mac Wellman has written over thirty plays, two novels, and several collections of poetry. Among his recent plays are 7 *Blowjobs* (performed at Soho Rep in New York and at San Diego's Sledgehammer Theatre); *Sincerity Forever* (commissioned by the Roger Nathan Hirsch Award for the Unicorn Theatre at the Berkshire Theatre Festival; and subsequently produced by BACA Downtown, New York, and at the Frank Theatre in Minneapolis); *Three Americanisms* (performed at the Soho Rep); *Crowbar* (performed at the Victory Theatre on 42nd Street in New York); *Bad Penny* (performed in Manhattan's Central Park as part of En Garde's Central Park Service); *Albanian Softshoe* (at the San Diego Rep); and *Terminal Hip* (also a solo piece for actor Steven Mellor, performed at P.S. 122 in New York). Wellman won a *Village Voice* Obie Award for *Bad Penny, Terminal Hip,* and *Crowbar* in 1990, and won another Obie for *Sincerity Forever* in 1991. In 1994 he won The America Award (The Ferns) for *The Hyacinth Macaw.*

Among his many drama publications are the recent collection of plays, *The Bad Infinity: Eight Plays,* published by Johns Hopkins University Press; *Bad Penny* and *The Professional Frenchman,* both published by Sun & Moon Press; and *Harm's Way,* published by Broadway Play Publishing. He has also edited several collections of plays, including *Theater of Wonders* (Sun & Moon Press) and 7 *Different Plays* (Broadway Play Publishing).

Wellman has also published several collections of poetry. *In Praise of Secrecy* (1977), *Satires* (1985), and *A Shelf in Woop's Clothing* (1990), among them. His novel, *The Fortuneteller,* was published by Sun & Moon Press in 1991.

He has received numerous grants, including awards from the McKnight and Rockefeller Foundations, and fellowships from the National Endowment for the Arts and the Guggenheim Foundation. He lives in Brooklyn with his wife, Yolanda Gerritson, a Dutch journalist.

AMERICAN THEATER IN LITERATURE (ATL)

Developed by The Contemporary Arts Educational Project, Inc., a non-profit corporation, and published through its Sun & Moon Press, the American Theater in Literature program was established to promote American theater as a literary form and to educate readers about contemporary and modern theater. The program publishes work of major American playwrights as well as younger, developing dramatists in various publishing programs of the Press, including the Sun & Moon Classics (collections of plays of international significance), and in collaboration with specific theater groups such as En Garde Arts, the Mark Taper Forum, Primary Stages, Soho Rep, and the Undermain Theatre.

BOOKS IN THIS PROGRAM

Len Jenkin *Dark Ride and Other Plays* ($13.95)
(Sun & Moon Classics: 22)

Robert Auletta *The Persians* ($9.95)
(A Mark Taper Forum Play)

Matthew Maguire *The Tower* ($8.95)

Kier Peters *The Confirmation* ($6.95)

Len Jenkin *Careless Love* ($9.95)
(A Soho Rep Play / Sun & Moon Classics: 54)

Mac Wellman *The Land Beyond the Forest: Dracula* AND *Swoop* ($12.95)

Mac Wellman *Two Plays: A Murder of Crows* AND
The Hyacinth Macaw ($11.95)
(A Primary Stages Play / Sun & Moon Classics: 62)

Jeffrey Jones *Love Trouble* ($10.95)
(An Undermain Theatre Play / Sun & Moon Classics: 84)

Jeffrey Jones and Jonathan Larson *J.P. Morgan Saves the Nation* ($9.95)
(An En Garde Arts Play / Sun & Moon Classic: 157)

David Greenspan *Son of an Engineer* ($8.95)

Matthew Maguire *Phaedra* ($9.95)
(A Creation Production Company / Home for Contemporary Theatre Book)

SUN & MOON CLASSICS

This publication was made possible, in part, through an operational grant from the Andrew W. Mellon Foundation and through contributions from the following individuals and organizations:

Tom Ahern (Foster, Rhode Island)
Charles Altieri (Seattle, Washington)
John Arden (Galway, Ireland)
Paul Auster (Brooklyn, New York)
Jesse Huntley Ausubel (New York, New York)
Luigi Ballerini (Los Angeles, California)
Dennis Barone (West Hartford, Connecticut)
Jonathan Baumbach (Brooklyn, New York)
Roberto Bedoya (Los Angeles, California)
Guy Bennett (Los Angeles, California)
Bill Berkson (Bolinas, California)
Steve Benson (Berkeley, California)
Charles Bernstein and Susan Bee (New York, New York)
Dorothy Bilik (Silver Spring, Maryland)
Alain Bosquet (Paris, France)
In Memoriam: John Cage
In Memoriam: Camilo José Cela
Rosita Copioli (Rimini, Italy)
Bill Corbett (Boston, Massachusetts)
Robert Crosson (Los Angeles, California)
Tina Darragh and P. Inman (Greenbelt, Maryland)
Fielding Dawson (New York, New York)
Christopher Dewdney (Toronto, Canada)
Larry Deyah (New York, New York)
Arkadii Dragomoschenko (St. Petersburg, Russia)
George Economou (Norman, Oklahoma)
Richard Elman (Stony Brook, New York)
Kenward Elmslie (Calais, Vermont)
Elaine Equi and Jerome Sala (New York, New York)
Lawrence Ferlinghetti (San Francisco, California)
Richard Foreman (New York, New York)
Howard N. Fox (Los Angeles, California)
Jerry Fox (Aventura, Florida)
In Memoriam: Rose Fox
Melvyn Freilicher (San Diego, California)
Miro Gavran (Zagreb, Croatia)

Allen Ginsberg (New York, New York)
Peter Glassgold (Brooklyn, New York)
Barbara Guest (Berkeley, California)
Perla and Amiram V. Karney (Bel Air, California)
Václav Havel (Prague, The Czech Republic)
Lyn Hejinian (Berkeley, California)
Fanny Howe (La Jolla, California)
Harold Jaffe (San Diego, California)
Ira S. Jaffe (Albuquerque, New Mexico)
Ruth Prawer Jhabvala (New York, New York)
Pierre Joris (Albany, New York)
Alex Katz (New York, New York)
Pamela and Rowan Klein (Los Angeles, California)
Tom LaFarge (New York, New York)
Mary Jane Lafferty (Los Angeles, California)
Michael Lally (Santa Monica, California)
Norman Lavers (Jonesboro, Arkansas)
Jerome Lawrence (Malibu, California)
Stacey Levine (Seattle, Washington)
Herbert Lust (Greenwich, Connecticut)
Norman MacAffee (New York, New York)
Rosemary Macchiavelli (Washington, DC)
Jackson Mac Low (New York, New York)
In Memoriam: Mary McCarthy
Harry Mulisch (Amsterdam, The Netherlands)
Iris Murdoch (Oxford, England)
Martin Nakell (Los Angeles, California)
In Memoriam: bpNichol
Cees Nooteboom (Amsterdam, The Netherlands)
NORLA (Norwegian Literature Abroad) (Oslo, Norway)
Claes Oldenburg (New York, New York)
Toby Olson (Philadelphia, Pennsylvania)
Maggie O'Sullivan (Hebden Bridge, England)
Rochelle Owens (Norman, Oklahoma)
Bart Parker (Providence, Rhode Island)
Marjorie and Joseph Perloff (Pacific Palisades, California)
Dennis Phillips (Los Angeles, California)
Carl Rakosi (San Francisco, California)
Tom Raworth (Cambridge, England)
David Reed (New York, New York)
Ishmael Reed (Oakland, California)
Tom Roberdeau (Los Angeles, California)

Janet Rodney (Santa Fe, New Mexico)
Joe Ross (Washington, DC)
Jerome and Diane Rothenberg (Encinitas, California)
Edward Ruscha (Los Angeles, California)
Dr. Marvin and Ruth Sackner (Miami Beach, Florida)
Floyd Salas (Berkeley, California)
Tom Savage (New York, New York)
Leslie Scalapino (Oakland, California)
Paul Schmidt (New York, New York)
James Sherry (New York, New York)
Aaron Shurin (San Francisco, California)
Charles Simic (Strafford, New Hampshire)
Gilbert Sorrentino (Stanford, California)
Catharine R. Stimpson (Staten Island, New York)
John Taggart (Newburg, Pennsylvania)
Nathaniel Tarn (Tesuque, New Mexico)
Fiona Templeton (New York, New York)
Mitch Tuchman (Los Angeles, California)
Paul Vangelisti (Los Angeles, California)
Vita Brevis Foundation (Antwerp, Belgium)
Hannah Walker and Ceacil Eisner (Orlando, Florida)
Wendy Walker (New York, New York)
Anne Walter (Carnac, France)
Jeffery Weinstein (New York, New York)
Mac Wellman (Brooklyn, New York)
Arnold Wesker (Hay on Wye, England)

If you would like to be a contributor to this series, please send your tax-deductible contribution to The Contemporary Arts Educational Project, Inc., a nonprofit corporation, 6026 Wilshire Boulevard, Los Angeles, California 90036.

SUN & MOON CLASSICS

AUTHOR   TITLE

Alferi, Pierre	*Natural Gaits* 95 ($10.95)
	The Familiar Path of the Fighting Fish 123 ($11.95)
Antin, David	*Selected Poems: 1963–1973* 10 ($12.95)
Barnes, Djuna	*At the Roots of the Stars: The Short Plays* 53 ($12.95)
	The Book of Repulsive Women 59 ($6.95)
	Collected Stories 110 ($24.95, cloth)
	Interviews 86 ($13.95)
	New York 5 ($12.95)
	Smoke and Other Early Stories 2 ($10.95)
Bernstein, Charles	*Content's Dream: Essays 1975–1984* 49 ($14.95)
	Dark City 48 ($11.95)
	Rough Trades 14 ($10.95)
Bjørneboe, Jens	*The Bird Lovers* 43 ($9.95)
	Semmelweis 137 ($10.95)
du Bouchet, André	*Where Heat Looms* 87 ($11.95)
	Today the Day 161 ($11.95)
Breton, André	*Arcanum 17* 51 ($12.95)
	Earthlight 26 ($12.95)
Bromige, David	*The Harbormaster of Hong Kong* 32 ($10.95)
Butts, Mary	*Scenes from the Life of Cleopatra* 72 ($13.95)
Cadiot, Olivier	*L'Art Poetic* 98 ($10.95)
Celan, Paul	*Breathturn* 74 ($12.95)
Céline, Louis-Ferdinand	*Dances without Music, without Dancers, without Anything* 129 ($12.95)
Coolidge, Clark	*The Crystal Text* 99 ($11.95)
	Own Face 39 ($10.95)
	The Rova Improvisations 34 ($11.95)

Copioli, Rosita	*The Blazing Lights of the Sun* 84 ($11.95)
De Angelis, Milo	*Finite Intuition* 65 ($11.95)
Deluy, Henri	*Carnal Love* 121 ($11.95)
DiPalma, Ray	*Numbers and Tempers: Selected Early Poems* 24 (11.95)
von Doderer, Heimito	*The Demons* 13 ($29.95)
	Every Man a Murderer 66 ($14.95)
	The Merowingians 113 ($15.95)
Donoso, José	*Hell Has No Limits* 101 ($12.95)
Dragomoschenko, Arkadii	*Description* 9 ($11.95)
	Xenia 29 ($12.95)
Eça de Queiroz, José Maria de	*The City and the Mountains* 108 ($12.95)
Eigner, Larry	*readiness / enough / depends / on* 185 ($12.95)
Federman, Raymond	*Smiles on Washington Square* 60 ($10.95)
	The Two-Fold Vibration 117 ($11.95)
Firbank, Ronald	*Santal* 58 ($7.95)
Fourcade, Dominique	*Click-Rose* 94 ($10.95)
	Xbo 35 ($9.95)
Freud, Sigmund	*Delusion and Dream in* Gradiva 38 ($13.95)
Gilliams, Maurice	*Elias, or The Struggle with the Nightingales* 79 ($12.95)
Giraudon, Liliane	*Pallaksch, Pallaksch* 61 ($12.95)
	Fur 114 ($12.95)
Giuliani, Alfredo, ed	*I Novissimi* 55 ($14.95)
Greenwald, Ted	*The Licorice Chronicles* 97 ($12.95)
Guest, Barbara	*Defensive Rapture* 30 ($11.95)
	Fair Realism 41 ($10.95)
	Seeking Air 73 ($12.95)
Hamsun, Knut	*Victoria* 69 ($10.95)
	Wayfarers 88 ($13.95)
	The Women at the Pump 115 ($13.95)
Hansen, Martin A.	*The Liar* 111 ($12.95)
Hardy, Thomas	*Jude the Obscure* 77 ($12.95)
Haugen, Paal-Helge	*Wintering with the Light* 107 ($11.95)

Hauser, Marianne	*The Long and the Short: Selected Stories* 138 ($12.95)
	Me & My Mom 36 ($9.95)
	Prince Ishmael 4 ($11.95)
Hawkes, John	*The Owl* and *The Goose on the Grave* 67 ($12.95)
Hejinian, Lyn	*The Cell* 21 ($11.95)
	The Cold of Poetry 42 ($12.95)
	My Life 11 ($9.95)
	Writing Is an Aid to Memory 141 ($10.95)
Hocquard, Emmanuel	*The Cape of Good Hope* 139 ($10.95)
Hoel, Sigurd	*The Road to the World's End* 75 ($13.95)
Howe, Fanny	*Radical Love* 82 ($21.95, cloth)
	The Deep North 15 ($9.95)
	Saving History 27 ($12.95)
Howe, Susan	*The Europe of Trusts* 7 ($10.95)
Jackson, Laura (Riding)	*Lives of Wives* 71 ($12.95)
James, Henry	*What Maisie Knew* 80 ($12.95)
Jenkin, Len	*Careless Love* 54 ($9.95)
	Dark Ride and Other Plays 22 ($13.95)
Jensen, Wilhelm	*Gradiva* 38 ($13.95)
Jones, Jeffrey M.	*J.P. Morgan Saves the Nation* 157 ($9.95)
	Love Trouble 78 ($9.95)
Katz, Steve	*43 Fictions* 18 ($12.95)
La Farge, Tom	*Terror of Earth* 136 ($12.95)
Larbaud, Valery	*Childish Things* 19 ($13.95)
Lins, Osman	*Nine, Novena* 104 ($13.95)
Mac Low, Jackson	*Barnesbook* 127 ($10.95)
	From Pearl Harbor Day to FDR's Birthday 126 ($10.95)
	Pieces O' Six 17 ($11.95)
Marinetti, F. T.	*Let's Murder the Moonshine: Selected Writings* 12 ($12.95)
	The Untameables 28 ($11.95)
Mathews, Harry	*Selected Declarations of Dependence* 128 ($10.95)

Messerli, Douglas, ed.	*50: A Celebration of Sun & Moon Classics* 50 ($13.95)
	From the Other Side of the Century: A New American Poetry 1960–1990 47 ($29.95)
	[and Mac Wellman] *From the Other Side of the Century II: A New American Drama 1960–1995* 170 ($29.95)
Morley, Christopher	*Thunder on the Left* 68 ($12.95)
Nerval, Gérard de	*Aurélia* 103 ($12.95)
Novarina, Valère	*The Theater of the Ears* 85 ($13.95)
North, Charles	*Shooting for Line: New and Selected Poems* 102 ($12.95)
Paradjanov, Sergei	*Seven Visions* 118 ($13.95)
Powell, Anthony	*Afternoon Men* 125 ($10.95)
	O, How the Wheel Becomes It! 76 ($10.95)
Propertius, Sextus	*Charm* 89 ($11.95)
Queneau, Raymond	*The Children of Claye* 92 ($13.95)
Rakosi, Carl	*Poems 1923–1941* 64 ($12.95)
Raworth, Tom	*Eternal Sections* 23 ($9.95)
Romero, Norberto Luis	*The Arrival of Autumn in Constantinople* 105 ($12.95)
Rosselli, Amelia	*War Variations* 81 ($11.95)
Rothenberg, Jerome	*Gematria* 45 ($11.95)
Sarduy, Severo	*From Cuba with a Song* 52 ($10.95)
Scalapino, Leslie	*Defoe* 46 ($11.95)
Schnitzler, Arthur	*Dream Story* 6 ($11.95)
	Lieutenant Gustl 37 ($9.95)
Steppling, John	*Sea of Cortez and Other Plays* 96 ($14.95)
Sorrentino, Gilbert	*The Orangery* 91 ($10.95)
Stein, Gertrude	*How to Write* 83 ($13.95)
	Mrs. Reynolds 1 ($11.95)
	Stanzas in Meditation 44 ($11.95)
	Tender Buttons 8 ($9.95)
	Three Lives 153 ($11.95)
Steiner, Giuseppe	*Drawn States of Mind* 63 ($8.95)
Streuvels, Stijn	*The Flaxfield* 3 ($11.95)

Svevo, Italo	*As a Man Grows Older* 25 ($12.95)
Taggart, John	*Loop* 150 ($11.95)
Thénon, Susana	*distancias / distances* 40 ($10.95)
Toufic, Jalal	*Oversensitivity* 119 ($12.95)
U Tam'si, Tchicaya	*The Belly* 143 ($11.95)
Van Ostaijen, Paul	*The First Book of Schmoll* 109 ($11.95)
Van Vechten, Carl	*Parties* 31 ($13.95)
Vesaas, Tarjei	*The Great Cycle* 133 ($11.95)
	The Ice Palace 16 ($11.95)
Waldrop, Keith	*Light While There Is Light: An American History* 33 ($13.95)
Walker, Wendy	*The Sea-Rabbit or, The Artist of Life* 57 ($12.95)
	The Secret Service 20 ($13.95)
	Stories Out of Omarie 56 ($12.95)
Watten, Barrett	*Frame (1971–1991)* 122 ($13.95)
Wellman, Mac	*The Land Beyond the Forest: Dracula* and *Swoop* 112 ($12.95)
	Two Plays: A Murder of Crows and *The Hyacinth Macaw* 62 ($11.95)
Wieners, John	*The Journal of John Wieners / is to be / called* 106 ($12.95)
Wilde, Oscar	*Salome* 90 ($9.95)
Zola, Emile	*The Belly of Paris* 70 ($14.95)